SHORT CUTS

INTRODUCTIONS TO FILM STUDIES

FANTASY CINEMA

IMPOSSIBLE WORLDS ON SCREEN

DAVID BUTLER

WALLFLOWER

LONDON and NEW YORK

A Wallflower Press Book
Published by
Columbia University Press
Publishers Since 1893
New York • Chichester, West Sussex
cup.columbia.edu

Wallflower Press® is a registered trademark of Columbia University Press

Cataloging-in-Publication Data is available from the Library of Congress

ISBN 978-1-906660-16-1 (pbk.)
ISBN 978-0-231-85141-1 (e-book)

Book and cover design: Rob Bowden Design
Cover image: *Pan's Labyrinth*. Picturehouse.

CONTENTS

For Stephen, Daniel, Janet, Richard, Scott, Rob and Simon or
Fistandantilus, Gren, Serena Olé, Teppich, Morg, Peregrin and Heinrick –
the finest adventurers the Old World has ever known

ACKNOWLEDGEMENTS

Major thanks first of all to Yoram Allon for backing this project and for his encouragement throughout. Thanks also to Jacqueline Downs and all at Wallflower Press. I am also indebted to the School of Arts, Histories and Cultures at the University of Manchester and my colleagues in the drama department for granting me a precious sabbatical in which to conduct archival research and get the writing process underway. Special thanks in this respect go to Alison Sharrock, Maggie Gale, Viv Gardner and Rajinder Dudrah. Once away I was helped massively by the ever generous staff at the British Film Institute library and, in particular, Janet Moat in Special Collections who identified relevant items that I would otherwise have been unaware of. A brief section of chapter 3 has appeared in a modified form in 'One Wall and No Roof Make a House: The Illusion of Space and Place in Peter Jackson's *The Lord of the Rings*', in Adam Lam and Nataliya Oryshchuk (eds) (2007) *How We Became Middle-earth*. Zollikofen: Walking Tree Publishers, 149–68.

I am extremely grateful for the encouragement and insight of Mark Astley, Chris Auld, David Berezan, Ricardo Climent, Laura Crossley, Emanuele D'Onofrio, Alexis Guneratne, Matthew Jones, Ming-Hsun Lin, Andy Murray, Mariano Paz, Ian Potter, Susan Rutherford, Johannes Sjöberg and Simon Smith. Much of this book has been trialled on and developed out of my course on adapting fantastic texts to film and so would not have been possible without the inspiration (and patience!) of all my students on the 'Falstaff and Gandalf' module – this book really is thanks to you all. It's not right to name names but the thoughts and contributions of Jennie Agg, Abigail Anketell-Jones, Stuart Brown, Stuart Burns, Sarah Crompton, Emily Davies, Esther Dennis, Sophie Falkner, Nicholas Garcia, Annie Gibson, Lisa Gill, Sapphire Goss, David Gray, David Hartley, Sophie

James, Emma Jones, Jessica Knappett, Carys Lavin, Amy Lewis, Benjamin Litherland, Rachel Littlewood, Hannah Mansell, Ali McDowall, Richard McGlashan, Lizzie Nurse, Jon Overton, Lauren Potts, Amy Ruffell, Eleanor Samson, Rebecca Tennenhaus, Rob Ward and Rachel Vipond have helped enrich the book and make writing it a pleasure. As always, my dearest thanks and love goes to my family – particularly Dad for walks in the fells (perfect for clearing the mind and thinking about space!) and Mum and Patrick for allowing me to take over the hayloft in order to finish the writing and bring the book safely home.

INTRODUCTION: THE PROBLEM OF FANTASY

It is 1933 and the *Daily Express* film critic, Cedric Belfrage (1933), has just been to see 'a marvel of screen entertainment', something that 'defies the laws of possibility, dares to try the impossible' and is a picture that 'everyone everywhere will want to see, even if it is only out of mere curiosity'. The name of the film, which Belfrage's contemporary, Paul Holt (1933), described in the *Daily Sketch* as 'the most fantastic that has ever been put on the screen', is *King Kong* (1933) and Belfrage is struggling to fulfil his duties as a critic:

> The voice of the critic might as well give itself a holiday in confrontation with this sort of picture ... You will hardly be human if you don't ask, How is it done? And I don't propose to tell you and spoil the illusion. Go and see it and enjoy it. Assume, if you like, that this is my underhand way of admitting that I have not got the foggiest idea myself how it is done. I am used to that sort of insult. (1933)

Belfrage was not alone amongst his peers in this kind of reaction. Writing in the *Daily Mirror*, R. J. Whitley (1933) considered the 'stupendous spectacle' of *King Kong* to be a picture which 'beggars description', whereas Holt's conclusion was that the film 'defies intelligent criticism'. For these writers, faced with such a fantastic construction as *King Kong*, the normal rules of critical engagement could no longer be applied. Reason was on the run from a 'fifty-foot' stop-motion ape. The result enabled the pressbook for the British release of *King Kong* to proclaim triumphantly:

> The Greatest Film the World will ever see
> Had the Greatest Press a Film will ever have

Critics outvie each other in
Finding new terms of praise. (Anon. 1933a)

This reaction by the British press to the original *King Kong* highlights some of the themes that will resurface throughout this book. The first is the notion that, irrespective of the dazzling wonders and alternative worlds on display, fantasy cannot or should not be subjected to meaningful critical analysis. It is a perception that has proven difficult to dispel. Some of the most popular and successful films of all time include fantasy films. The variety of fantasy filmmaking takes in everything from much-loved classics like *A Matter of Life and Death* (1946) and *Mary Poppins* (1964), cult pictures such as *Conan the Barbarian* (1982) and *Krull* (1983), to 'arthouse' films by heavyweights of world cinema such as Federico Fellini (*Giulietta degli spiriti* (*Juliet of the Spirits*, 1965)) and Ingmar Bergman (*Fanny och Alexander* (*Fanny and Alexander*, 1982)), with a tonal range stretching from low-key and understated depictions of the fantastic (such as *Otoshiana* (*Pitfall*, 1962)) to big-budget extravaganzas (*The Lord of the Rings* (2001–03)). Yet fantasy's dominant image, fairy tales for children or pulp sword and sorcery for adolescents, does not do justice to the diversity of approaches to fantasy in film.

Fantasy is all too often dismissed as child's play beyond serious study. The origins of this critical antipathy towards fantasy, in Western thought at least, go back a long way. Kathryn Hume traces the roots to Plato and Aristotle, and their advocating of an analysis of literature that focused purely on its mimetic qualities at the expense of anything veering into the fantastic realm of centaurs, gorgons or 'countless other strange monsters'. As Hume summarises, the consequences of this position have been far-reaching:

> Plato may have approved fantasy in some guises, since he entrusted important ideas to its images, but his negative views are the ones to have influenced later generations ... Tasso, for instance, mentions flying horses, along with enchanted rings and ships turned into nymphs, as permissible for the ancients, but a breach of decorum for his contemporaries ... David Hume disparages literary fantasy as a threat to sanity. (1984: 6)

This negativity towards fantasy would not disappear in the twentieth century.

Lucie Armitt's observation that 'it takes only a small step not just to connect fantasy with "popular" rather than "serious" literature, but actually to presume that the terms fantasy fiction and formula fiction are simple synonyms for each other' (1996: 1) is just as applicable to the critical reception of fantasy in film if not all the arts. In his study of fantasy film, Joshua David Bellin refers to Brian Attebery's address to the 1995 International Conference on the Fantastic in the Arts as being indicative of critical attitudes towards fantasy:

> The title of his talk – 'The Politics (If Any) of Fantasy' – and its tone indicated his sense that he was broaching a subject quite unprecedented, even heretical, to the majority of his listeners: 'The politics of fantasy – what a peculiar thing to talk about! ... what has politics got to do with it?' (2005: 4)

Not unrelated here is the prevailing perception of fantasy, whether cinematic or literary, as being 'mere' escapism without any meaningful content or social function. Thomas Schatz, for example, dismisses film fantasy sweepingly and denies it any potential for political relevancy with his assertion that 'we see films that are increasingly plot-driven, increasingly visceral, kinetic, and fast-paced, increasingly reliant on special effects, increasingly "fantastic" (and thus apolitical)' (1993: 23). I will return to the question of escapism in the final chapter but it is worth noting here that, for many critics sympathetic towards fantasy, the charge of escapism (and it is most often couched in negative terms rather than the possibility that escapism might also be a constructive and necessary function) has been a frustrating one that has persisted stubbornly. Indeed, Alec Worley's critical survey of fantasy film identifies the task of overthrowing this one perception as being among its core aims:

> If this survey could banish any single misconception about the fantasy genre (and there are dozens to choose from), it would be the idea that fantasy amounts to nothing but meaningless escapism. This lie oozes so much honey that the genre itself is often smitten. So let's clear this one up right away. Fantasy is inextricably defined by reality; how else can one define what doesn't exist except by what does? (2005: 4)

Both Rosemary Jackson and Lucie Armitt, in their respective studies of literary fantasy, affirm fantasy's presence at the heart of human creativity. For Armitt, fantasy is 'central to all fictional work' (1996: 1) and, as Jackson notes, the fantastic 'derives from the Latin, *phantasticus* ... which is from the Greek meaning to make visible or manifest. In this general sense, all imaginary activity is fantastic, all literary works are fantasies' (2003: 13). 'Imaginary activity' can be extended, of course, far beyond the creative arts to include the fields of science, technology, politics and so on. The basic principle of fantasy, imagining a world different to the one we know, is at work in the act of speculation and every time we ask the question 'what if?', whether that is followed by the statement 'dragons roamed the air', 'we could land on the moon', 'poverty was eliminated' or 'a cure for cancer was found'. To be sure, fantasy can be manifest (and sometimes splendidly so) in the most lurid and populist of forms, seemingly free of social relevance, but it is a much more fundamental activity than a marginalised genre aimed at a narrow demographic. For J. R. R. Tolkien, fantasy was nothing less than a basic human right (see 2001: 56).

The second recurring theme is the relationship between fantasy and spectacle. The emphasis on spectacle has not always been beneficial to fantasy film, whether in terms of the commissioning and production of fantasy film projects or the perception of fantasy film by audiences, critics and those within the film industry. As we have already seen with *King Kong*, the focus on stunning visuals has often resulted in less attention being given to the actual content, by filmmakers as well as critics, but the spectacular 'wonder picture' has remained the dominant model for the mainstream fantasy film, in Hollywood at least. Many of the earliest fantasy films of significance, such as *Die Nibelungen* (1924), *The Thief of Bagdad* (1924) or *The Wizard of Oz* (1939), were lavish and ambitious films in which spectacle was to the fore, yet the attendant cost of creating these extraordinary worlds would have been a deterrent to an industry for which financial success is of prime importance. None of these films gave rise to a sustained wave of live-action fantasy films in the years immediately following their release. The notion that fantasy necessitated spectacle on a grand scale, coupled with difficult socio-economic conditions (the US Depression of the 1930s and World War Two), meant that it never became a dominant presence in the era of classical filmmaking. By the late 1990s, according to *The Lord of the Rings*' executive producer Mark Ordesky, the film industry had pronounced fantasy as being 'dead or dormant' (quoted in Spector 2005: 59).

It is difficult, however, to make the same claim about fantasy films in the 2000s. Writing about *The Lord of the Rings*, Ian Hunter has asserted that 'since the late 1970s the dominant genre of Hollywood blockbusters has been fantasy' (2007: 154). Hunter's comment, seemingly at odds with Ordesky's, underlines the difference that often exists between academic and industry perspectives and interpretations of fantasy (a third recurring theme in this book). This location of the upswing in fantasy's fortunes as being in the late 1970s is perhaps a little premature, as a result of its fusion of fantasy with science fiction (the riddle of genre cannot be evaded and I will address the distinction between fantasy and science fiction in chapter 1). Yet although I would suggest that science fiction tended to hold the upper hand throughout the 1980s and 1990s with the major blockbusters being science fiction franchises such as the *Terminator* films (1984–2003), *Back to the Future* (1985–90), the *Jurassic Park* series (1993–2001), *The Matrix* trilogy (1999–2003) and individual titles such as *Independence Day* (1996), Hunter's general principle nonetheless holds true. Not only have fantasy films in the 2000s enjoyed major box-office success but there has also been belated recognition from the film industry that fantasy is not just a vehicle for special effects and merchandising opportunities targeted at a juvenile audience. At the 2004 Academy Awards, *The Return of the King* (2003), the final instalment of Peter Jackson's sequence of films based on Tolkien's *The Lord of the Rings*, won all eleven of the awards that it was nominated for. This exceptional haul was significant not just because it equalled the record for the most Academy Awards won by a single film (shared with *Ben Hur* (1959) and *Titanic* (1997)) but, as several news agencies noted at the time, it also included the award for best picture: the first time a fantasy film had won that category. Was this victory an indicator that attitudes towards fantasy were changing?

On the surface, fantasy film would indeed appear to be experiencing something of a golden age. For Western cinema, the pivotal year was 2001. Not only did the end of 2001 see the release of the first part of *The Lord of the Rings*, *The Fellowship of the Ring*, but it also witnessed the first instalment of the other fantasy film series to triumph at the box office throughout the 2000s, *Harry Potter and The Philosopher's Stone*. If they were the most famous, these films were not, however, the only fantasy-themed productions to succeed financially in 2001. Jeffrey Spaulding's overview of the year's grosses noted the qualities shared by these films:

> Almost every major had at least one such success story this year, and each adhered to many of the same elements as *Harry Potter* and *Lord of the Rings*. The common threads seem to be a PG or PG-13 rating (a film for the entire family) and elements of fantasy (special effects or animation). The money is spent on making the film look spectacular rather than on salaries for big stars ... DreamWorks had its piece of the action with *Shrek* ... Disney hit the jackpot with *Monsters, Inc.* ... Fox scored with *Planet of the Apes* and *Dr. Dolittle 2*, Paramount with *Lara Croft: Tomb Raider*, and Miramax with *Spy Kids*. (2002: 55)

Spaulding's summation of 2001 underlines the emphasis in contemporary Hollywood fantasy on spectacle and a non-adult or family audience but also confirms the resurgence of fantasy filmmaking. This resurgence has not been limited to Hollywood. In France, where, as Guy Austin observes, the emphasis on directors over genres has meant that, despite notable contributions from filmmakers such as Georges Méliès, Jean Cocteau and Georges Franju to Jean-Jacques Beineix, Luc Besson and Leos Carax, 'the fantastic has been perceived as a principally Anglo-Saxon form' (2008: 143), since 'around 2000, a new generation of fantasy filmmakers has sprung up' (2008: 144) with films such as *Le Pacte des loups* (*The Brotherhood of the Wolf*, 2001) 'triumphant proof that the French fantasy film has finally come back to life' (2008: 164).

The *Lord of the Rings* and *Harry Potter* series went from strength to strength and, by 2005, Susan Napier would commence her study of Japanese *anime* with the observation that 'in the last few years, fantasy in general has roared back into a prominent place in popular culture' suggesting that the success of *Harry Potter* and *The Lord of the Rings* revealed 'a global hunger for fantasy' (2005: xi). For Napier, this 'yearning' for fantasy has come about (in part) as a result of a shift away from the technological trappings and focus of science fiction, combined with a reaction to specific and troubling circumstances:

> The reasons behind this yearning are no doubt diffuse, but it seems safe to say that the last decade of the twentieth century ushered

in an increasing disaffection with technology ... Problems such as
environmental degradation, economic downturns, and war appear
increasingly intractable, with science seeming to suggest little in
the way of overall solutions. In addition, in America at least, the
events of September 11 have cast a long shadow over the national
psyche. It is little wonder that fantasy worlds offering alternatives
to the frightening new reality should become increasingly popular.
(2005: xi)

A charge of escapism is easily made here but in her analysis of Hayao
Miyazaki's *Mononoke-hime* (*Princess Mononoke*, 1997), Napier discusses
how the alternative worlds presented by some fantasies need not necessarily be a safe haven that the spectator can run to in order to shelter from
the stresses and difficulties of contemporary society. Far from denying
issues such as 'cultural dissonance, spiritual loss, and environmental col-
lapse', Miyazaki's film, argues Napier, foregrounds these tensions in contemporary Japan and uses fantasy 'to disturb or problematize our notions
of reality' (2005: 242).

The shift from science fiction to fantasy has also been observed by
Marina Warner, albeit much earlier than Napier. Speaking at the British
Film Institute in February 1992, Warner identified 'an extraordinary resurgence of interest in fantasy and romance' (1993b: 77) and noted Terry
Gilliam's transition from the science fiction fantasy of *Brazil* (1985) to the
reworked medieval romance of *The Fisher King* (1991) as being a significant indicator of fantasy's renewal. As one of the leading exponents and
explorers of fantasy in contemporary cinema, Gilliam might not have been
the best example as evidence of a sudden resurgence in fantasy's fortunes: he would return to science fiction with *Twelve Monkeys* (1995) and
his free-wheeling imagination had taken him into the realm of fantasy and
fairy tale prior to *Brazil* with *Jabberwocky* (1977) and *Time Bandits* (1981).
A recurring theme in much of Gilliam's work however, irrespective of its
predominant genre, is the act of fantasising and inventing alternate realities. Kevin, Sam Lowry, Baron von Munchausen, Parry, L. J. Washington,
Raoul Duke and Dr. Gonzo, the Brothers Grimm, Jeliza-Rose and, most
tantalisingly for Gilliam, his 'unfinished' Don Quixote: all of these characters from different Gilliam films are fantasists or delusional in one way
or another. For some, their fantasies are (self) destructive (Sam in *Brazil*);

7

for others, fantasy is a means of making sense of and surviving in their world (Jeliza-Rose in *Tideland* (2005)); Gilliam has addressed the seductive dangers of fantasy as well as its healing and liberating qualities. His approach to fantasy is thus not a straightforward paean to escapism and in this sense his films are often in keeping with Warner's suggestion, as part of a discussion on the 'old wives' tale', as to the reasons for fantasy's renaissance:

> There can be a Utopian impulse behind all of this; it can be a way of telling an alternative story, of sifting right and wrong according to a different voice, and a voice that is perhaps disregarded, discredited or neglected ... In times of crisis, of fragmentation and violence, romancing can serve a richer purpose than escapism. The critic Gillian Beer has written, in a wonderful essay on romance which goes back to this medieval form: 'Romance, being absorbed with the ideal, always has an element of prophecy. It remakes the world in the image of desire.' ... The possibilities of romance thus include the possibility of altering inherited prejudices and stock figures. (Ibid.)

The use of voices previously disregarded, discredited or neglected is a feature of several of Gilliam's revisionist (fairy) tales, not least in *Tideland* with its emphasis on two unconventional central characters in the form of Jeliza-Rose (Jodelle Ferland), a pre-pubescent girl who administers her father's heroin and loses both parents to overdoses, and Dickens (Brendan Fletcher), a childlike lobotomised adult, both of whom employ fantasy in order to cope with the adverse conditions of their lives. Alone in an isolated landscape, Jeliza-Rose's use of fantasy, faced with the reality of her father's rotting corpse around which she strives to construct some kind of life, is very much in keeping with Ernst Bloch's assertion that 'stage and story can be either a protective park or a laboratory ... they can be a flight from or a prefiguring of the future' (quoted in Zipes 1988: xxvi). As with Guillermo del Toro's *El Laberinto del fauno* (*Pan's Labyrinth*, 2006), winner of three Academy Awards in 2007 as well as the BAFTA for Best Film not in the English Language (and thus another indicator of fantasy's burgeoning contemporary fortunes), the portrayal of a girl's fantasy world is far from sentimental: *Tideland* ends with a devastating train crash and *Pan's Labyrinth*, set in fascist Spain at the end of World War Two, with its juvenile fantasist, Ofelia (Ivana Baquero), being shot by her callous step-father. Both these films exemplify Rosemary Jackson's summation of the modern fantastic, drawing on the work of Fredric Jameson, as being a subversive form, non-nostalgic and unsentimental (unlike the fantasy of so much of Disney's output), but representative of 'dissatisfaction and frustration with a cultural order which deflects or defeats desire' (2003: 180). In Gilliam's case, *Tideland* was motivated, in part, by a frustration with the way contemporary Western culture, in his view, has victimised children and denied them any meaningful agency or capacity for resilience. Del Toro's targets in *Pan's Labyrinth* also include the treatment of children by society, with the creatures encountered by Ofelia being representations or transformations of 'political power' and the faceless pale man, with eyes lodged in the stigmata on his hands, embodying 'the church and the devouring of children' (del Toro quoted in Kermode 2006b: 23). For Jackson, the genuine fantastic (and what is meant by that will be the focus of chapter 1) 'desires transformation and difference' (2003: 179) and this transformative potential of fantasy, whether in terms of the characters and situations within the text or the spectator's own perceptions and worldview, will be discussed at greater length in the final chapter, which considers the social function of fantasy and contrasting responses to it.

If the success of films such as *Pan's Labyrinth* and *The Lord of the Rings* suggests a contemporary landscape more sympathetic towards fantasy, fantasy nonetheless remains under suspicion and often misunderstood by the

Fantasy as manifestation of institutional power: the faceless man in *Pan's Labyrinth* (2006)

film industry and its critics. Some of the most revealing pieces of evidence in this respect are Peter Jackson's comments, before *The Lord of the Rings* had been released, about the fantasy films of the 1980s, one of the few periods of sustained fantasy filmmaking in Western cinema, principally in the form of sword and sorcery, heroic fantasy or barbarian pictures such as *Hawk the Slayer* (1980), *The Beastmaster* (1982), *Krull* or *Red Sonja* (1985). In an Internet question and answer session with Harry Knowles of the *Aint It Cool* website, Jackson addressed the legacy of these films in response to Knowles' question 'in the last twenty years the fantasy film has nose-dived into granite. What is wrong with the modern fantasy film?'

> One of my chief reasons for wanting to spend nearly five years of my life making these films has been that I don't think that fantasy has been well-served by cinema. So I agree with your comments. I can't get into a deep debate about the last twenty years of fantasy, but I have been disappointed by the films as well. Either the style has been wrong, or often the scripts have been terrible. Starting out with strong scripts (and we are obviously dealing with great material) will put us ahead of a lot of other fantasy films. Not making the movies self-consciously fantasy will help too. (Quoted in Knowles 1998)

Jackson identified *Willow* (1988), a late entry in the 1980s wave of heroic fantasy films, as typifying the failings of the 'modern fantasy film' and the kind of approach to the portrayal of fantasy worlds that *The Lord of the Rings* would purposefully steer away from. However different to our known world, Jackson sought to invest his vision of Tolkien's Middle-earth with diegetic depth and authenticity as well as a sense of historicity that would extend beyond the events portrayed on screen:

> It might be clearer if I described it as an historical film. Something very different to *Dark Crystal* or *Labyrinth*. Imagine something like *Braveheart*, but with a little of the visual magic of *Legend*. It should have the historical authority of *Braveheart*, rather than the mean-ingless fantasy mumbo-jumbo of *Willow*. (Quoted in Knowles 1998)

The extraordinary attention to diegetic coherency and intricate detail in the films' *mise-en-scène* are clear markers of the success of Jackson and his army of collaborators in overcoming the spectre of 1980s fantasy but *The Lord of the Rings* has not necessarily resulted in a host of epic fantasy films following in its wake. As the writer and producer Dean Devlin has suggested:

> I actually think that *Lord of the Rings* has made it tougher to get original fantasy or sci-fi films made, because studios think the success of those films proves their theory that films in the genre have to be based on an established property ... It's still very expensive to make these movies, so they are reluctant, and only want to do the ones that they think are safe. (Quoted in Spector 2005: 60–1)

Devlin's assessment of the state of contemporary fantasy filmmaking is certainly supported by the films which were released or entered production in the aftermath of the success of *The Lord of the Rings* and *Harry Potter* franchises. *Hauru no ugoko shiro* (*Howl's Moving Castle*, 2004),*The Chronicles of Narnia: The Lion, the Witch and the Wardrobe* (2005), *Gedo senki* (*Tales from Earthsea*, 2006), *Eragon* (2006), *Bridge to Terabithia* (2007), *The Dark is Rising* (2007), *Stardust* (2007), *The Golden Compass* (2007) – all of these (not necessarily Hollywood) films are adaptations of existing fantasy properties.[1] Such a focus on pre-existing literary sources makes the success of an original fantasy script like *Pan's Labyrinth* all the more notable.

Written, produced and directed by Guillermo del Toro, *Pan's Labyrinth* has been described by Mark Kermode (2006a) as 'a transformative, life-affirming nightmare ... a *Citizen Kane* of fantasy cinema'. Kermode's praise is sincere but the invocation of the magic words '*Citizen Kane*' and its accompanying allure as 'the greatest film ever made' is intriguing. Despite having a tradition that can be traced back to the earliest years of cinema and the impossible journeys of Georges Méliès in particular, there is still a lingering need to contextualise and justify fantasy in relation to the accepted canon of classics. The underlying inference perhaps is that, prior to *Pan's Labyrinth*, fantasy had yet to reach a maturity and level of filmmaking that could produce a masterpiece comparable to Orson Welles' film in terms of a unified vision of form and content. It is unfair to Kermode, who has been a great champion of the supernatural and fantastic in film, to scrutinise the reference to *Citizen Kane* (1941) so closely but the implications are of interest here (irrespective of whether one shares the opinion about the respective merits of *Citizen Kane* and *Pan's Labyrinth*). For better or worse, the shadow of childhood and suggestion that it is a genre only just emerging from its infancy continues to loom large over fantasy and how it is perceived and discussed.

Where film studies is concerned, the discussion of fantasy has been somewhat compromised. Although science fiction and horror have received extensive coverage through articles such as Robin Wood's 'The Return of the Repressed' (1978) and numerous book-length studies (such as Clover (1992), Telotte (1995) and Jancovich (1996)) or edited collections (such as Kuhn (1990 and 1999) or Redmond (2004)), fantasy film does not yet have a comparable literature. Certain branches of fantasy film have enjoyed considerable attention (such as Arthurian cinema and fairy tales) but fantasy film as a whole lacks the range of critical discussion afforded science fiction and horror.

There are several 'encyclopaedias' or directories of fantasy (such as Senn & Johnson (1992), Clute & Grant (1997)) but few in-depth critical studies. Kenneth Von Gunden's *Flights of Fancy: The Great Fantasy Films* (1989), for example, offers little analysis and is more an account of production processes whereas James Donald's edited collection, *Fantasy and the Cinema* (1989), is indicative of much academic work on fantasy: the use of the term to discuss films from other/overlapping genres. In Donald's opening section, 'The Cinefantastic', which seeks to explore the fantastic as a 'genre or mode', three of the four essays are studies of the horror film and the fourth is a focus on German Expressionist cinema, emphasising horror again. This 'squeezing out' or displacement of fantasy in favour of horror and science fiction is a recurring feature of much of the literature from the 1980s and is perhaps best encapsulated by the Autumn 1982 issue of *Film Criticism*. The editorial, by J. P. Telotte, sets out the issue's impressive intentions, which include the bracketing of 'the phenomenon of horror within the larger category of fantasy' and the use of the term film fantasy as 'an indicator of a trait or character which a number of distinct genres share and which imparts to them a commonality that cuts across the boundaries of such formulas as horror, science fiction, and heroic adventure' (1982a: 2–3). The range of films discussed, however, does not quite fulfil the editorial's welcome promise of inclusiveness. Also, the issue's cover, where 'HORROR' towers over 'AND FANTASY' (not unlike those adverts emblazoned with 'SEX!' only to be followed by 'now that we've got your attention' and something that the authors fear the reader will deem less interesting), is revealing of prevailing concerns in film studies at that time.

One of the problems facing the study of fantasy is the diversity of meanings attached to the word and their various applications. The *Oxford English Dictionary*, for example, provides seven contrasting meanings, several of which have negative connotations that have contributed to the critical antipathy towards fantasy. These range from liking or desire to a whim or 'changeful mood', a supposition with no solid grounds or a delusional imagination and extravagant or visionary fancy. The film scholar faces other questions. Does fantasy refer to an identifiable genre or a mode? If it is a genre, how should it be defined and its parameters be set? In the academic literature, fantasy as a term has often been used in relation to how films express *our* fantasies and desires regardless of genre and whether anything in the film's diegesis disrupts our understanding of mimesis and what is possible in our known world. To give one recent example, Mark Fisher's critique and analysis of Lacanian themes in *Basic Instinct 2* (2006) discusses how the 'infamous leg-crossing scene' of the first *Basic Instinct* (1992) articulates the desire at the core of the film: 'was this a female fantasy of a woman subduing men with her sexuality and confidence, or was it a male fantasy of abasement before a dominatrix?' (2007: 76). The fantasies mentioned by Fisher are not impossible in the strictest sense (they do not break what is empirically and physically possible in our world, although they are perhaps unlikely in terms of what is *socially* possible – i.e. the restrictions of family and what is perceived as acceptable behaviour mean that most of the police officers watching Catherine Tramell (Sharon Stone) will almost certainly not get to abase themselves before such a figure, however much they might desire to), opening up a different approach to the concept. The roots of this psychoanalytical work can be found in Sigmund Freud's understanding of fantasy. For Freud, writing in the late nineteenth century, fantasy was a psychic process and one related directly to the repression of traumatic memories. Fantasy constructs were a means of negating or soothing the pain of the past. As Vicky Lebeau's overview of Freud summarises:

> Fictions, daydreams, are conjured by a subject who feels the need
> for protection. Fantasy intervenes. It comes between the self and

its history, consciousness and reality – making use of things seen, heard, and experienced to rework the world. (2001: 29)

Once again, fantasy is associated with escapism, motivated by a desire to escape from a troubling past or distressing present – but not necessarily into an impossible world. J. P. Telotte has noted the potential consequence of a focus on desire *per se* as being a detour away from the fantastic towards other genres and impulses ('that way lies either pornography or voyeurism' (1982b: 57)) but desire, nonetheless, remains central to much fantasy, or 'wish-landscapes' as Ernst Bloch might have phrased it, not least through one of fantasy's most familiar tropes: transformation (whether via a magic lamp, wand, potion, ring, handful of beans or whatever). For Slavoj Žižek, it is through fantasy that 'we learn how to desire' (1991: 6). James Donald (1989) employs Jean Laplanche and Jean-Bertrand Pontalis's psychoanalytical understanding of fantasy as the '*mise-en-scène* of desire' (Laplanche & Pontalis 1988: 318) and, similarly, Telotte argues that 'a crucial attraction of the fantasy film is not simply the fear or awe it commonly inspires in viewers, but the images of desire it raises' (1982b: 57). Telotte's article addresses the figure of the double in fantasy but, again, the case studies are drawn from horror (*Frankenstein* (1931)), science fiction (*Blade Runner* (1982)) or fusions of the two (*Invasion of the Body Snatchers* (1956)). Elsewhere, Michael Ryan and Douglas Kellner (1988) include a chapter on 'fantasy films' in their study of the manifestation of ideology in contemporary Hollywood cinema but, once more, the category is applied loosely with their examples (such as *THX 1138* (1971), *Logan's Run* (1976) and *Outland* (1981)) all relating to science fiction (fear of machines and loss of social freedom in a future dystopia). I have laboured this point not as a criticism of the writers mentioned above. Donald, Telotte, Ryan and Kellner all have extremely valuable things to say, which can be applied to the genuine fantasy film, but the curious fact remains: fantasy films have often been absent from the discussion of fantasy in film. Much depends, of course, on how one understands and classifies the category but the task of compiling an effective bibliography on cinematic fantasy is not a straightforward one.

Joshua David Bellin's *Framing Monsters: Fantasy Film and Social Alienation* (2005) provides a rare extended study of fantasy film. Taking in *King Kong*, the *Arabian Nights* adventures of Ray Harryhausen, dragons and mutants, Bellin shifts the study of fantasy from the emphasis on psychoanalysis to a consideration of the ways in which fantasy films have harboured and expressed social fears and ideological values. A welcome addition to the available literature on cinematic fantasy, although emphasising fantasy's perceived harmful effects, Bellin's focus on ideology critique refers to both narrative content and, albeit to a lesser extent, visual style. In doing so, *Framing Monsters* manages to avoid one of the pitfalls and recurring traits of much scholarly discussion of fantasy in film. As Michael Klossner summarises in his overview of the literature on horror and fantasy film:

> William Paul adds 'It is one thing to claim that horror films deal with the return of the repressed, as Robin Wood has, and to find the repressed to signify sexual material. Still, we may consider just how the horror film deals with this.' Too many academic studies have neglected the 'how' in pursuit of the 'why'. (1999: 530)

This study aims to provide an introduction to the study of fantasy film that addresses both form and content, outlining formal approaches to the fantastic from a range of cinemas (not just Hollywood) as well as an awareness of the contexts in which they are produced and engaging critically with the issues they raise. Chapter 1 outlines definitions of fantasy before focusing on the changing use of the term by the film industry. Chapter 2 considers several of the major genres of fantasy film, including the fairy tale film, *Arabian Nights* adaptations and sword and sorcery. Chapter 3 addresses the concern that many studies of cinematic fantasy neglect detailed discussion of *how* these films operate and are constructed. The chapter explores the methods used by filmmakers to create an effective sense of the fantastic and portray fantasy worlds on screen, ranging from atypical approaches to editing, camera movement and shot composition to the crucial use of sound and music to augment the nature of what we see. The final chapter discusses the social function of fantasy and the often conflicting interpretations of particular films. Building on the themes raised here, this final chapter details attitudes towards fantasy including those of critics who have seen fantasy film as either a source of conservatism and harmful beliefs or have championed the potential of fantasy to be socially progressive, regenerative or subversive. Via a case study of

John Boorman's *Excalibur* (1981), the chapter considers how, irrespective of authorial intent, fantasy films have been claimed to mirror our actual world and appropriated by audiences from often opposing movements and political viewpoints.

The term 'fantasy film' has been applied inconsistently by academics, critics and the industry. It is the source of such a diverse range of films, one contributed to by such unlikely kindred spirits as Pier Paolo Pasolini, Walt Disney, Andrei Tarkovsky and Ray Harryhausen, that the desire to explore the fantastic through film is clearly far more than an exercise in joining a series of semantic and syntactic dots. At a time when fantasy is flourishing on our screens, we need to be wary of generalised interpretations such as fantasy being nothing more than innocent escapism (if these films do offer escapism, what are they providing an escape route from and to?) or, conversely, the default home of subversive challenges to existing social structures and ideologies. We all engage in fantasy at some point in our lives, and not just in childhood, but as critics and students of film we have been enchanted indeed if we take these films for granted and allow them to slip away unchecked.

1 ESTABLISHING FANTASY: DEFINITIONS AND DEVELOPMENTS

What is a fantasy film? Do fantasy films constitute a genre? How much fantasy does a film need to contain to be considered a fantasy film? The answers to these questions can vary depending upon whom you ask. Put the question about fantasy's generic status to a representative of the film industry and you might receive a straightforward 'yes'. Although never a dominant presence in terms of the actual number of films released, fantasy has been used by the film industry and its related trade press as a means of classifying a film in terms of genre for some time. Fantasy is one of the categories used by the UK Film Council in its annual genre classification audit of films released in the UK, with the other categories being, in the 2004 survey for example, action, adventure, animation, biopic, comedy, crime, documentary, drama, family, horror, music, musical, romance, science fiction, thriller and war.[1] Outside the UK, as Steve Neale notes, fantasy is one of the 61 categories used by the American Film Institute in its 'Genre Index' of 1930s feature films and was used by trade press titles such as *Motion Picture Herald* in the 1930s (see 2000: 242). Similarly, Rick Altman refers to a 1944 internal document for the Motion Picture Producers and Distributors Association in which Will Hays compiled a list of the principal 'types and kinds of feature-length films' that ran as follows: melodrama, western, drama, crime, comedy, musical comedy, horror, documentary, fantasy and travelogue (see 1999: 109–10).

But put the same question about whether fantasy can be considered a genre to a film academic and you are likely to receive an answer in the negative. Tellingly, Neale's expansion of Richard Maltby's eight major genres (the western, comedy, musical, war film, thriller, crime/gangster film, horror and science fiction) to 14 (adding the detective film, epic, social problem film, teenpic, biopic and action-adventure into the mix) has no place for fantasy (see 2000: 51). Neale is not alone in this respect. Fantasy is barely mentioned in Altman's extended study of genre and not at all in Barry Keith Grant's (2007) introduction to the subject or Wheeler Winston Dixon's collection of essays on 'the dominant popular genres of the 1990s' (2000). Neale is careful to acknowledge that the terms used by critics, theorists and the industry (as well as its relay) have 'generally coincided' but that 'anomalies and problems remain' (2000: 51). Fantasy is clearly such an anomaly.

Fantasy and genre

The reason for fantasy's absence from most critical studies of genre is because, taken as a whole, the term embraces too many types of film to be accommodated by the prevailing theoretical approaches to genre classification. As Rosemary Jackson notes, quoting Eric Rabkin (1976: 118), at the outset of her study of literary fantasy:

It seems appropriate that such a protean form has so successfully resisted generic classification. 'The wide range of works which we call ... fantastic is large, much too large to constitute a single genre. [It includes] whole conventional genres such as fairy tale, detective story, Fantasy'. (Jackson 2003: 13)

Where film is concerned, if we take as a starting place Barry Keith Grant's statement that 'genre movies are those commercial feature films which, through repetition and variation, tell familiar stories with familiar characters in familiar situations' (2007: 1) then the problem facing fantasy becomes clear. Fantasy contains numerous sub-genres that correspond comfortably with Grant's definition: heroic fantasy (such as *Willow*, *Eragon*), the *Arabian Nights* film (*The Thief of Bagdad* (1940), *The Golden Voyage of Sinbad* (1974)) or the ghost film (*The Ghost and Mrs Muir* (1947),

Ghost (1990)) are all fantasy-related genres or types of film with recurring settings, character types and narrative situations. But finding the shared familiar elements between these sub-genres is less straightforward. What are the familiar elements that unite *Eragon* and *The Ghost and Mrs Muir*? The settings could not be more dissimilar: the magical 'fierce and beautiful' kingdom of Alagaësia in the former and a small coastal town in late Victorian England in the latter. The central characters are also markedly different: an orphaned farm boy destined to become a Dragon Rider and, in Lucy Muir (Gene Tierney), an independent widow and mother. On the surface there does not appear to be much that is familiar to each film.

Even if we adopt a more analytical approach to genre classification such as Rick Altman's semantic/syntactic model, the two films remain generically distant. For Altman, an effective study of genre should consider both a film's semantic elements (i.e. its visual iconography and themes, 'common topics, key scenes, character types, familiar objects, recognisable shots and sounds' (1999: 89)) and its syntactic features, which comprise the way in which its various structural elements combine to create meaning (an approach that, Altman suggests, can provide an 'understanding of textual workings and deeper structures underlying generic affiliation' (ibid.), such as plot structure, character relationships or image and sound montage). We have already addressed, briefly, some of our two featured films' semantic elements but the differences continue at the level of plot structure and character relationships. *Eragon* follows a familiar pattern of the heroic adventure narrative whereas *The Ghost and Mrs Muir* is a romance, charting Lucy's often spiky relationship with Captain Daniel Gregg (Rex Harrison). At a very basic structural level, although it could be argued that each film adheres to the classical pattern of order/disorder/ order restored, there are distinct contrasts between the two. *Eragon* is the more formulaic as the boy Eragon (Ed Speleers) gains his powers and overcomes a series of difficulties before triumphing at the end with the promise of further adventures ahead. *The Ghost and Mrs Muir*, however, for all its charm, has a more sombre tone as Lucy is separated from the Captain, enters into a slow and patient decline, and is only reunited with him at the very end in death. In addition to their tonal difference, the films are also aimed at different audiences with *Eragon* targeted at a family/teenage demographic (the film is based on a series of books written by a teenager, Christopher Paolini), or as the *Guardian* film critic Peter Bradshaw put it somewhat more acerbically, 'an interminable Jackson-Tolkienian fantasy for boys, whose enjoyment levels will be in direct relation to testicle-height' (2006) and *The Ghost and Mrs Muir* being a tender 'weepie' aimed at an older female audience. There is virtually no generic compatibility between the two films and they are united in fantasy only by virtue of the fact that Captain Gregg is a deceased seaman and Lucy's slow-burning love affair is with a ghost.

The principle that binds *Eragon* and *The Ghost and Mrs Muir* to the category of fantasy is their divergence from what is possible in our known world. Even then, *Eragon* is far more overt in this respect with its kingdom full of wizardry and creatures such as dragons being an accepted part of this secondary world. *The Ghost and Mrs Muir*, conversely, has only one fantasy element (if we discount Gene Tierney's English accent) but one that is central to the whole film: Captain Gregg's undead condition. What the two films share then is an approach to reality that enables them to correspond to the fourth meaning of fantasy provided by the *Oxford English Dictionary*: 'Imagination; the process or the faculty of forming mental representations of things not actually present' and its offshoot 'a product of imagination', which might be a story or film or painting and so on. But such a definition, as we have established, is not the basis for a coherent genre and the result of this definition has been that fantasy, as Jackson notes, 'has been applied rather indiscriminately to any literature which does not give priority to realistic representation' (2003: 13).

The divergence from what is possible in our known world, of course, is just as much a feature of science fiction and horror, so in what way is fantasy distinct? As we saw in the introduction, for a number of film scholars, such as Telotte (1982a) or Ryan and Kellner (1988), fantasy is used as a term referring to a 'trait or character which a number of distinct genres share' (Telotte 1982a: 2) but that inclusiveness has not prevented other critics and theorists from attempting to construct boundaries between these related non-mimetic idioms. Horror is arguably the easiest of the three to isolate through its emphasis on generating a specific emotional response in its audience, whereas fantasy and science fiction are not as locked into any one such reaction (feelings of awe and wonder may predominate but they are not essential). The distinction between fantasy and science fiction, however, is more hazy. In his 1947 study of German film, Siegfried Kracauer described *Metropolis* (1927) as an example of the 'then current machine cult' and Fritz Lang's interest in 'technical fantasies' (2004: 149). Although written when both the popular and critical understanding of science fiction and fantasy was vastly different to our own – indeed, the actual phrase 'science fiction' was still relatively young if we accept Hugo Gernsback's assertion that he invented the term for the magazine *Amazing Stories* in the late 1920s – Kracauer's use of 'technical fantasies' is indicative of the tendency for fantasy and science fiction to often be conflated into a single category. One consequence of this conflation, however, has been the desire for certain critics to create 'purified' bodies of work. This desire is most evident in the critical work on science fiction and is perhaps best expressed in the writing of Darko Suvin.

Fantasy, Suvin and estrangement

Derek Littlewood's observation that Suvin sought to 'vomit the fantastic out of the body of SF' (quoted by Parrinder 2000: 38) may seem like a strongly-phrased assertion but it is in keeping with Suvin's own statements.[2] As Patrick Parrinder highlights, Suvin's project, begun in a series of essays written in the 1970s, has been to establish a poetics of science fiction that would be a way of 'asserting the genre's literary respectability [and] presenting it as a suitable object for criticism and theory' (2000: 37). The need to rid science fiction of the perceived toxin of fantasy is one of the most revealing examples of the critical antipathy towards fantasy with the idiom being unwelcome to what we might think of as one of its kindred spirits. For Suvin, however, genuine science fiction was distinct from fantasy through its emphasis on the process of cognition. Science fiction, fantasy, myth, fairy tale – whatever the variant – all operate from the same basic premise which is an 'imaginative framework alternative to the author's empirical environment' (Suvin 1979: 7). This alternate reality, asserts Suvin, creates a sense of estrangement as the reader/spectator/ character in the text is confronted with a world contrary to the one that they know. But where science fiction departs from the 'Great Pumpkin antics of fantasy' (Suvin quoted in Parrinder 2000: 38) is the extent to which it attempts to explain or rationalise its estranging elements and enable the reader/spectator to make cognitive sense of the empirical differences. Suvin's definition of science fiction is thus founded on the tension between cognition and estrangement, which is generated by the presence of a *novum* ('new thing'), whether that is an unfamiliar lifeform, artefact, environment or process. From a Suvinian perspective, fantasy is less concerned (if at all) with any cognitive requirements and its estranging qualities receive little rationalisation or credible explanation: they simply happen and are accepted (or not, if one is a character like Alice refusing to accept the nonsensical behaviour of the inhabitants of Wonderland) within their fictional world.

There is still plenty of room for slippage here. A film such as *Flash Gordon* (1980), with its bright and vivid worlds of Mongo overseen by the Emperor, Ming the Merciless, might have a planetary system accessed via spaceships and feature other forms of remarkable technological hardware, but these can be thought of as kingdoms, winged horses and magic swords given new clothes; the narrative has no interest in their workings or their social/philosophical implications. This semantic pretence of dressed-up iconography is barely hidden in a film such as *Krull* where a space-travelling alien overlord known as The Beast materialises his lair/ship (the Black Fortress) on a pseudo-medieval planet, lets loose his army of Slayers, who blast laser bolts from their weapons and abduct a princess just prior to her wedding, before The Beast is undone by an eccentric fellowship led by the brave Prince Colwyn. The cursory nods and name-checking of science fiction iconography (space travel, energy weapons, hostile aliens) are such that both *Flash Gordon* and (less so) *Krull* qualify as examples of science fantasy, a sub-genre which, Parrinder notes, Suvin was particularly suspicious of as 'under the guise of cognition the ancient obscurantist enemy infiltrates [science fiction's] citadel' (quoted in Parrinder 2000: 38).

But if the portrayal of advanced technology in a film does not guarantee any meaningful degree of cognition then, by the same token, works of overt fantasy should not necessarily be assumed to be devoid of attempts to activate the cognitive process. Although not concerned with any scientific or technological attempts at rationalising his secondary world, Tolkien's body of work set in and around Middle-earth goes to extraordinary lengths to establish a coherent geography, functioning languages, alphabets, detailed histories and mythic cycles for his various races. The diegetic depth and mimetic rigour available to Peter Jackson from Tolkien's work provided the director with the kind of material that he sought in order to encourage the audience to accept Middle-earth and avoid the aforementioned 'mumbo jumbo' fantasy worlds of films such as

Willow. The first instalment of *The Lord of the Rings, The Fellowship of the Ring* (2001), opens with an extensive prologue that establishes the lengthy back-story to the three films ahead, introducing key figures such as Isildur, Elrond and Sauron, whose actions will have major consequences in the later films even though they themselves have little actual onscreen time (it is Isildur's weakness, for example, and failure to destroy the Ring in the prologue that, centuries later, burdens Aragorn's conscience, filling him with self-doubt, and thus making for a more psychologically interesting character than a conventional uncomplicated hero archetype). For Jackson, the time spent constructing a believable world is clearly a necessary strategy if the audience are going to commit to such lengthy films and develop an emotional involvement with the characters and issues. Jackson may have singled out *Willow* but other films could have been selected as examples of possessing what Yvonne Tasker refers to as 'mock mythologies' (1993: 28) typical of 1980s sword and sorcery, such as *Conan the Destroyer* (1984) and *Red Sonja.* The effect of these mock mythologies and the way they are often undercut by characters within the film, argues Tasker, is a 'doubleness ... around a tacit acknowledgement of the hilarity with which the narratives, which take themselves seriously, are actually received' (ibid.). *The Lord of the Rings* is not quite the sole exception that proves the rule about fantasy's lack of concern for creating believable and internally consistent alternative worlds. Films such as *Dragonslayer* (1981) and *The Dark Crystal* (1982) imbue their fantasy societies with an internal logic and sense of a wider functioning world that marks them out from the carefree romps of many of their contemporaries – albeit at the expense of narrative momentum in the case of *The Dark Crystal. The Lord of the Rings*, nonetheless, does demonstrate the considerable effort required for a fantasy film to convey such an in-depth and convincing secondary landscape.

Used uncritically then, Suvin's emphasis on the dialectic between cognition and estrangement can result in some surprising admissions to and exclusions from the category of science fiction. Carl Freedman (2000) provides excellent examples of the dangers inherent in Suvin's definition before demonstrating how it can be applied effectively. As Freedman notes, to some extent, *all* fiction deals with cognition and estrangement. With that in mind one might regard a writer such as Bertolt Brecht, who specialised in alienation techniques, to be more worthy of science fiction status than a film like *Star Wars* (1977), which makes abundant use of familiar tropes and archetypes (drawn from westerns, samurai films, ancient myth and so on). There is not much cognitive estrangement at work in *Star Wars* whereas Brecht excels in estrangement. Is *Star Wars* thus to be considered fantasy and Brecht a neglected master of science fiction? As Freedman clarifies:

> The term of science fiction ought to be reserved for those texts in which cognitive estrangement is not only present but dominant. Brecht is indeed an author in whose work the SF tendency is not only strong but dominant. Masterpieces like *Mother Courage* (1941) are essentially thought experiments ... [But Brecht is] relatively uninterested in those specifically *technological* versions of estrangement that have traditionally figured (though to a decreasing degree since the 1960s) in science fiction that derives directly from the pulp line. Conversely, *Star Wars* might be understood as activating the science fiction tendency only weakly and fitfully in most regards ... but with a spectacular hypertrophy of the specifically *visual* dimension associated with science-fictional tales of space travel. Both Brecht and [George] Lucas, then, might be described as producers of science fiction, but in quite different ways, which a dialectical generic approach allows us to specify with some precision. (2000: 22; emphasis in original)

Fantasy, Todorov and hesitancy

If Suvin established through his poetics of science fiction what fantasy was not, then his contemporary in the 1970s, Tzvetan Todorov, produced a similarly influential definition that was addressed specifically at fantasy and the fantastic in particular. Todorov's work remains one of the most oft-cited studies of (literary) fantasy although, as with Suvin, it is not without its complications (see Bould 2002: 51–7). Just as Suvin's model creates an effective 'scale' of science fiction, with 'hard' science fiction at one end and science fantasy at the other, Todorov's definition of the fantastic employs a schema in which there are several distinctive sub-categories or registers of fantasy. For Todorov (1975), the fantastic is a specific form of fantasy and does not just refer to any collection of non-naturalistic or supernatural events and characters. Goblins, wizards, magic carpets and purple people eaters do not qualify automatically and can be comfortably contained within the obviously unreal realm of the marvellous. The genuine fantastic, argues Todorov, is much more subversive than the marvellous: it is the uneasy space where one can no longer be certain about what is real or unreal. Todorov identifies two related categories of fantasy, the marvellous and the uncanny, with the fantastic occupying the inexplicable centre-ground between them. The marvellous is reserved for the clearly supernatural and genuine magic. The uncanny (discussed at length by Freud in his 1919 essay on the subject) is comprised of those instances where, ultimately, a natural explanation can be offered in which all strangeness is generated by unconscious forces (our own psyche). Then there is the fantastic, in which no conclusive explanation can be found. Crucial to the fantastic therefore is the presence of hesitancy, as Todorov asserts:

> The text must oblige the reader to consider the world of the characters as a world of living persons and to hesitate between a natural and supernatural explanation of the events described. Second, this hesitation may also be experienced by a character; thus the reader's role is entrusted to a character ... the hesitation is represented, it becomes one of the themes of the work. (1975: 33)

As Rosemary Jackson, who expands Todorov's work by considering the psychoanalytical dimensions of the fantastic, notes, fantastic narratives:

> Pull the reader from the apparent familiarity and security of the known and everyday world into something more strange, into a world whose improbabilities are closer to the realm normally associated with the marvellous. The narrator is no clearer than the protagonist about what is going on, nor about interpretation; the status of what is being seen and recorded as 'real' is constantly in question. (2003: 34)

Todorov's schema is a useful way of distinguishing between different registers of fantasy and a means for identifying recurring formal properties and thematic concerns. Yet, as Kathryn Hume has observed (see 1984: 19–20), in its attempt to define fantasy and the fantastic in specific terms,

Todorov's work is ultimately exclusive and, like that of Suvin, is less effective in dealing with texts that slip in and out of genres and registers or exist on the periphery of what might be considered fantasy. In its application, as with much structuralist criticism of its era, it is all too easy to reduce Todorov's definition into a tool to be used in a game of classification without engaging more fruitfully with a text's wider socio-historical context, theoretical implications and contrasting audience reception (as Lucie Armitt, who uses Todorov as the basis for her own work on literary fantasy, reflects, 'so much ground has been lost in comparison with other fields of literary criticism while critics of fantasy have been futilely squabbling over whether a text is marvellous or fabulous, or how to subdivide science fiction into space opera or sword and sorcery' (2000: 13)).

Todorov's definition of the fantastic, as being a text which generates or articulates hesitancy, establishes clear-cut parameters for the genre but, as Hume notes (see 1984: 14), few texts sustain such a hesitant tone throughout. The same is certainly true, if not more so, of mainstream cinema, which is geared towards a strong sense of narrative closure and clarification of any unresolved issues, leaving the inexplicable and uncertain nature of Todorov's fantastic at odds with dominant filmmaking traditions such as the storytelling codes of the classical Hollywood model (an 'excessively obvious' cinema as David Bordwell, Janet Staiger and Kristin Thompson (1985) have described it). For the vast majority of its duration, *Cat People* (1942), one of the distinctive sequence of horror/fantasy-related films produced by Val Lewton for RKO, would appear to fit perfectly with Todorov's criteria (unlike the 1982 remake). Directed by Jacques Tourneur and with evocative cinematography by Nicholas Musuraca, the film relies on shadowplay and sound effects (necessitated by budgetary limitations) as well as acting and *mise-en-scène* to *suggest* its fantasy element, right up until the final act. The central enigma relates to the character of Irena Dubrovna (Simone Simon), a Serbian-born fashion designer, who believes she is descended from the people of a cursed medieval village and will transform into a panther whenever she is angered or sexually aroused. With a psychiatrist character present to provide rational explanations for Irena's fears, counter-balanced by an impressive audio-visual ambiguity in memorable sequences such as Irena's stalking of Alice and the swimming pool, the film seems committed to not revealing its hand: Irena may well just be deluded by a folk memory and the sexual jealousies and anxieties of the main characters provide the fuel for their perception of their surroundings taking on an uncanny quality. As a result, *Cat People* is psychological drama rather than an overt supernatural thriller – at least until Irena's ultimate transformation and attack on the psychiatrist at the end of the film, a creative decision that Tourneur opposed, taking the film away from Todorov's hesitancy and underlining the strong pull in mainstream cinema towards narrative clarity, whether in a prestige production or a B picture such as *Cat People*.

An example of a film that exemplifies Todorov's definition of the fantastic would be *The Innocents* (1961), Jack Clayton's film of Henry James' *The Turn of the Screw* (1898). James' novella is one of the texts highlighted by Todorov in his study and the film maintains the unease over whether the central character (James' nameless governess becomes Miss Giddens (Deborah Kerr) in the film) is really experiencing the supernatural (have the two children in her care been possessed?) or is projecting her unconscious fears and desires onto the world around her instead: by the end of the film we are left without any answers and only our own conclusions. Neil Sinyard refers to one of Kerr's letters in which she underlined Clayton's commitment not to dispel the aura of mystery:

'I remember asking Jack [Clayton] what he wanted me to stress in playing the part', Kerr wrote, 'and he replied: "You play it the way you feel, but don't forget the ambiguity!" So I tried the very nervous tight-rope between sanity and insanity, and left the audience to exercise its intelligence'. (Quoted in Sinyard 2000: 88)

The film's distinctive approach to portraying the supernatural ('a strange new experience in SHOCK' announced the pressbook (Anon. 1961a)) was not lost on critics at the time. *Variety*'s label of 'off-beat psychological drama' (Anon. 1961b) indicates a hesitancy on the part of the critic over how to clearly categorise the film – more obvious genre categories such as horror or ghost film cannot be employed so easily. This uncertainty over what kind of film *The Innocents* was and how it should be promoted (respectable costume drama or populist chiller?) would complicate the film's distribution and reception. Clayton's expertly sustained ambiguity resulted, ultimately, in a critically well-respected film: François Truffaut left Clayton a note describing *The Innocents* as 'the best English film after Hitchcock goes to America' (quoted in Sinyard 2000: 81). However, few film-

Hesitancy in *The Innocents* (1961)

makers in large-budget mainstream cinema would dare to leave audiences so uncertain as to the nature of what they had just spent their money on. The following review of *The Innocents*, posted to the film's discussion board on the Internet Movie Database, is indicative of the potential hostility available to a film that might leave too much to the audience's imagination:

I was recommended this movie. I wanted to be scared, and i [sic] can't handle the gore of a ton of newer movies, and really dig old horror movies, but this was just terrible. Went in with high expectations, kept saying it was gonna [sic] be awesome, suspense kept building and building and ... now it's over? The movie could have been cut down from 100 to 60 minutes, and then complete the extra 40 with an actual ending. No resolution at all. Ok, so the ghost isn't possessing the kid anymore ... and that means not just him, but BOTH of the ghosts are gone now? And isn't that other girl still possessed? That Quint guy willingly took himself out of the kid, and there's no way he would've done that if it would've conquered him ... It kept building it's [sic] terror, and never climaxed at all. I jumped maybe once. Good one, Innocents. (TheMrFraz 2007)

Such a reaction suggests perhaps why, in terms of mainstream cinema, Todorov's definition of the fantastic has tended to be identifiable only momentarily within a film rather than accounting for a substantial corpus of 'wholly' fantastic works. Given the financial imperatives of the film industry, it is not surprising that the emphasis, in Hollywood at least, has been on a different sort of fantasy.

Fantasy violence

If Todorov's account of the fantastic has tended to remain an academic definition by critics for critics, how has the film industry used and understood fantasy as a category? In recent years, fantasy has been employed increasingly as a means of classifying a film in terms of the audience that is allowed to see it, via cautionary advice such as 'contains fantasy violence'. This categorisation of 'fantasy violence' follows the revision of parental guidelines implemented by the US television industry in 1997. The new rating system included two categories for children's programming: TV-Y (programmes suitable for all children) and TV-Y7 (programmes suitable for older children) with the option of a further descriptor, FV, to denote the portrayal of 'fantasy violence' in the programme. The FV descriptor has since been taken up by both the film and video game industry as a means of differentiating product and offering advice to parents concerned about the content of a film or game. Once again, fantasy is used in relation to something being less real and thus, perhaps, not to be taken as seriously, the inference being that FV is (more) acceptable violence. What constitutes fantasy violence, however, and the point at which it ceases to be 'fantasy' is unclear. Aragorn's (Viggo Mortensen) decapitation of the Uruk captain, Lurtz (Lawrence Makoare), in the battle at the end of *The Fellowship of the Ring*, for example, is a spectacular moment of screen violence. The violence is 'clean' – there is no blood (an imposition placed on the filmmakers to meet censorship concerns) – and the victim is 'acceptable' – Aragorn is acting in self-defence against an evil monster who has just slain one of his comrades. But the act remains one in which the spectator is encouraged to take pleasure (not least through the purity of Aragorn's strike and the *absence* of any blood – it is constructed as both an aesthetically and dramatically pleasing act) and the tone of the battle is played for real (in keeping with the realism Jackson sought to invest the film with elsewhere).

The *Lord of the Rings* films provided the fantasy violence category with one of its sternest tests and the extended DVD releases would contain additional violence deemed potentially excessive for a theatrical release, for which a substantial family audience would be vital if the franchise was to be a financial success. The British Board of Film Classification (BBFC) gave *The Fellowship of the Ring* a PG (Parental Guidance) rating (and 12A ratings – meaning nobody younger than 12 could see the film unless accompanied by an adult – for the subsequent instalments in the trilogy) with the additional advice that the film's 'battle violence and fantasy horror may not be suitable for under 8s'. This was adjusted to 'intense' combat and battle violence for the next two films. The consequences for a big-budget film like *The Fellowship of the Ring* to be categorised in such a way that made it inaccessible to children would be potentially catastrophic, not only in terms of its box-office performance but also the vast array of related tie-in merchandise, including toys. For some then, fantasy violence, rather than offering clear guidance to parents, has been interpreted instead as a convenient 'get out clause' for an industry nervous about loss of revenue. Writing at the time the FV descriptor was first introduced by US television, Joanne Cantor, who has extensively researched the effects of the mass media on children and teen audiences, observed that:

[The] industry's insistence on euphemisms, rather than describing content clearly and accurately, is a major complicating factor ... they balked at using the word 'violence' to refer to the mayhem that goes on in many children's shows, such as 'Power Rangers' or 'The X-Men'. Instead, they use the letters 'FV' to refer to 'fantasy violence' – whether the violence is indeed of the impossible variety or whether it is quite realistic but simply performed by animated characters. In the case of both 'D' [situations where sex is talked about] and 'FV', the change was insisted upon by the industry to reduce the possible loss of advertising revenue they expected the word 'sex' on the one hand, or 'violence' on the other, would cause. (1997)

Aragorn's removal of Lurtz's head complicates the two categories of fantasy violence referred to by Cantor ('impossible' or 'quite realistic but simply performed by animated characters', where we might replace 'animated' with 'non-mimetic'). It is not 'impossible', in that a strong sword-strike to the neck is likely to result in a fatal injury, and the live-action characters and their performances are presented with a tone of gritty realism (even if one of the combatants is a monstrous humanoid) that makes them not so easy to dismiss as 'simply ... animated characters'.

The effect of the absence of blood has contentious results. In one sense, it meets the requirements of the US ratings system implemented by the Motion Picture Association of America (MPAA), which stipulates that a film with intense action violence may receive a PG-13 rating but that the

'It's only a flesh wound': fantasy violence in *The Fellowship of the Ring* (2001)

violence will generally not be 'both realistic and extreme or persistent' and thus blood is less likely to be on display, whereas the next rating levels (R and NC-17 (no one under the age of 17)) can accommodate more extreme and graphic portrayals. But is the denial or softening of the portrayal of violence healthier for an impressionable younger audience than a violent act whose consequences are clearly understood? Media effects research is extensive and violence is one of the most studied aspects. Craig Anderson's co-authored study 'The Influence of Media Violence on Youth' concludes that 'the extant research literature clearly reveals that exposure to violent media plays an important causal role in violence in modern society' (Anderson *et al.* 2003: 105). Anderson is careful to acknowledge that the nature of this role is complex and shaped by a diverse range of social and psychological factors as well as the formal properties and narrative context of the onscreen violence. In a separate summary of 'all the scientific studies that have examined the effects of television violence', Edward Donnerstein (n.d.) suggests that a portrayal of violence that 'poses the greatest risk for the learning of aggression' would contain the following, all relating to the violence being made more 'palatable' and justifiable:

- An attractive perpetrator
- Morally justified reasons for engaging in aggression
- Repeated violence that seems realistic and involves a conventional weapon
- Violence that is rewarded or goes unpunished
- No visible harm or pain to the victim
- A humorous context

Aragorn's duel and decapitation of Lurtz corresponds to the majority of Donnerstein's factors. There is even an element of grotesque humour as Lurtz's right arm is severed cleanly, as if made of plasticine, and he pulls Aragorn's sword deeper into his own chest, almost gloating over Aragorn's inability to kill him, only to lose his head. Narrative context is a mitigating factor – the film has established that its heroes are not indestructible (neither Gandalf (Ian McKellen) or Boromir (Sean Bean) make it safely to the end) and violence is seen to have serious consequences, but there is a fusion in the beheading scene of mimetic and non-mimetic elements, which creates an oscillation between what is understood as real and unreal that could prove potentially confusing for young children. As Donnerstein notes, 'research shows that children under the age of 7 have difficulty distinguishing reality from fantasy ... what seems unrealistic to a mature viewer may appear to be quite real to a younger child'. Donnerstein's collation of studies of violence in the media is, however, only concerned with the hazardous effects of screen violence on children. A contrasting argument that suggests screen fantasy violence can have a beneficial effect can be found in the 2002 court brief presented by a group of 33 leading screen and media academics (including Martin Barker, Henry Jenkins and Vivian Sobchack), which was delivered as a response to a court decision in St Louis to ban young people from access to video games perceived to be too violent. In summarising the function of fantasy violence, the brief stated:

> [Henry] Jenkins describes at least four functions of violent enter-tainment: offering youngsters 'fantasies of empowerment', 'fan-tasies of transgression', 'intensification of emotional experience', and an acknowledgement that the world is not all sweetness and light' ... Experts on childhood and adolescence have long recog-nised the importance of violent fantasy play in overcoming anxie-ties, processing anger, and providing outlets for aggression. Bruno Bettelheim was a pioneer in describing these responses in the context of violent fairy tales. As film historian John Lewis explains, Bettelheim understood that children have 'terrible struggles, terri-ble fears'; they are 'small, and fully aware that they have no power'. (Various 2003 [2002]: Part 4, Section III)

The court brief would prove a success (although not without criticism – see, for example, Kline (2003)) and the lower court order banning the video games was overturned. The debate about media effects and the impact of screen violence on young audiences, however, has not abated. It is not the intention of this study to attempt a definitive conclusion on the issue, but what I hope is clear by now is that the descriptor 'fantasy violence' is an ambiguous one, derived in part by mixed motives (the need to offer parents better advice compromised by the financial fears of the industry) and open to contrasting interpretations and agendas. The effectiveness of the term depends in many ways on one's understanding of the word 'fantasy' but, as we have seen, that word has a far from stable definition and application.

The wonder film

Long before the term 'fantasy violence' appeared as a means of rating a film, fantasy was used by the film industry and its attendant press to categorise films more conventionally in relation to genre. As far back as 1924, Raoul Walsh's *The Thief of Bagdad*, produced by and starring Douglas Fairbanks, emphasised its generic status in its opening title card, unashamedly proclaiming that the film was 'An *Arabian Nights* Fantasy'. This use of fantasy by the industry as a genre category has not been consistent (just a year after *The Thief of Bagdad*, *Variety* struggled to categorise the dinosaur adventure *The Lost World* (1925) as anything other than 'a most unusual picture' (Anon. 1925)) and the term has slipped in and out of regular use. An overview of the generic labels applied to earlier films that we might now classify as fantasy is revealing, not just in relation to shifting terminology but also attitudes towards fantasy as a category. Although the Walsh/Fairbanks *The Thief of Bagdad* identified itself as fantasy, in Britain, another term was applied to the film that would be used throughout the 1920s and 1930s to describe pictures that we would now include within the category of fantasy: the 'wonder film'.

Reviews on both sides of the Atlantic lavished *The Thief of Bagdad* with praise and a wide variety of superlatives. For some, it was more than just a film – it realised the true potential of the medium, raised it to new heights and, in certain extreme reactions, was considered to be proof of the cultural sophistication of an entire nation. *The New York Sun* asserted that the film should be filed away 'in a bronze reel case in the hollow of a keystone that will show some prying generation of the future how far Americans came in ingenuity and sensitiveness' (Anon. 1984). Following the film's appearance at the Theatre Royal, Drury Lane, London critics were equally entranced and the film's UK Exploitation and Publicity Campaign Book summarised the critics' reaction as being to 'universally' hail the production as 'the wonder film' (Anon. 1924a). Extracts from a host of glowing reviews were highlighted: 'let it be understood at once that here is a screen play like none other. All that I had hoped someone might dare to do with the film is here dared, successfully' marvelled the *Evening Standard* (ibid.). Described variously as a 'glorious fantasy', 'marvellous fairy tale' and 'wonderful love story', the use of the term 'wonder film' or 'wonder tale' seems to have been applied in relation to audience reaction – audiences, quite literally, wondered how these spectacles were achieved. As the reviewer of the *Daily Chronicle* commented, 'every new scene is a revelation of artistic composition and of technical miracle' (ibid.). The programme for the film's screening at the Theatre Royal included a section titled 'How Are They Done?' (but did not offer any answers) and the Campaign Book provided tantalising snippets of details about the film's 'mechanical wonders,' which ranged from the magic flying carpet and the winged horse to the crystal realm and the valley of monsters (ibid.). Fantasy, adventure and romance were used by the Campaign Book as adjectives to describe the film but the advice to the potential viewer was clear. In order to entice prospective viewers, the Campaign Book encouraged exhibitors to approach local shopkeepers to 'make a special window display of gaily coloured cushions', and so on, after the Oriental style.[3] The window card should read:

It was on Cushions like these,
THE THIEF OF BAGDAD lounged.
See this Wonder Film at ... (Ibid.)

Following the success of *The Thief of Bagdad*, Fritz Lang's two-part epic fantasy *Die Nibelungen* was screened at the Royal Albert Hall, also to enthusiastic reviews ('a production of extraordinarily attractive beauty' said the *Times*, whereas the *Daily Mail* was of the opinion that the film was 'artistically the most ambitious ever yet seen in this country. It raises the art of the kinema to a higher plane' (Anon. 1924b), apparently leaving *The Thief of Bagdad* dethroned in a matter of months). Once more, the tag of 'wonder film' was employed to describe the production, with the emphasis on its technical achievement.

Not surprisingly, this association with extraordinary spectacle and special effects ensured that *King Kong* would also be described as, among many other things, a wonder film (and within the film's own diegesis, Kong is titled the 'Eighth Wonder of the World'). The review in *Variety* underlined the reaction of many: 'while not believing it, audiences will wonder how it was done' (Anon. 1933b). In this sense, audiences are far from passive in their consumption of a film such as *King Kong*. Drawing on the work of

Philip Fisher (1988), Michelle Pierson proposes that the wonder generated by visual effects 'makes thought a component of aesthetic experience, returning to it an incitement to curiosity and contemplation that it has not always been credited with' (2002: 21). *King Kong* was the featured presentation at the launch night of The Troxy, tellingly dubbed 'London's Latest Wonder Theatre', which opened on 11 September 1933, with *King Kong* dwarfing all other films in the theatre's souvenir programme. The film's impact is still evident in the press material that circulated around its later re-releases: the pressbook for the 1938 re-release championed the film as 'the most successful percussion adventure fantasy yet conceived and produced by man' and urged audiences to 'see this wonder adventure once more' (Anon. 1938). Two years later, 'wonder film' was still being used as a category to promote fantasy-related films with the release of 'Alexander Korda's Technicolor spectacle' *The Thief of Bagdad* (1940), described in the Exhibitors' Campaign Book as 'The Wonder Picture of the Year!' (Anon. 1940). By 1946, the marvels of *A Matter of Life and Death*, including its giant mechanical staircase spanning time and space, resulted in a US poster campaign that described the film as 'a motion picture beyond all wonder!' In the publicity surrounding these spectacular films, audiences are often encouraged to wonder and puzzle at how the effects are achieved but, like most magicians, the filmmakers do not reveal too many of their secrets. As the Campaign Book for the 1924 version of *The Thief of Bagdad* put it, 'several authorities have asked for scientific explanations of some scenes but these must be left unexplained for the present' (Anon. 1924a).

'Wonder film' was used less and less as a category throughout the 1940s and 1950s, with *The 5,000 Fingers of Dr T* (1953) billed as 'the wonder musical of the future', being a late example. 'Wonder film', of course, is not a phrase familiar to film audiences in the early twenty-first century. Although the remarkable innovations of films such as *2001: A Space Odyssey* (1968) and *Star Wars* would rekindle that response for their generation, we have an increasing *lack* of wonder at visual effects: we know so much about the production process, now more than ever, through the exposure of press junkets, making-of books and documentaries, DVD featurettes and commentaries, so that we might be impressed by a spectacular effect but are less likely to *wonder* about how it was achieved when the default answer is a piece of computer-generated imagery. In terms of our understanding of film production, the 'wonder film' belongs to a much more innocent age.

Fantasy as generic category in the film industry

Where was the term 'fantasy' at this time? As we have seen, fantasy was used by the industry but there was often uneasiness about foregrounding it as a film's generic dominant. *The Wizard of Oz* was marketed as MGM's 'Technicolor musical fantasy' with the musical element tending to be emphasised far more in the promotional posters than the fantasy aspect. In a piece called 'Fantasy Comes to the Screen', the official press-book claimed that the film was the first to combine successfully 'adult and juvenile appeal in a motion picture fantasy' noting in a separate item that this successful reaching out to adults and children was achieved by virtue of an engaging plot, clever dialogue, lilting songs, amusing lyrics and a 'philosophy which will never be forgotten' (Anon. 1939a). If *The Wizard of Oz* was aimed at adults and children, thus making its fantasy elements a more acceptable part of its promotional material, then fantasy was a more uncomfortable presence in the press material surrounding an adult-oriented film such as *It's a Wonderful Life* (1946). The film's pressbook noted that 'drama, comedy, romance and fantasy are the ingredients of Frank Capra's new production' but fantasy was missing from the taglines created for the film – 'Frank Capra's new romantic comedy', 'a delightful romantic drama', 'romantic comedy drama', 'an emotional comedy drama, packed with human interest' and 'an emotional drama of life' (Anon. 1946). The pressbook referred to a review of the film by the *Chicago Daily Tribune*, which reassured its readers that 'it is fantasy but gracefully handled' in case they were concerned about the film's 'overtones of fantasy' (as the film's official synopsis described them) getting out of control and resulting in a distasteful picture. There is a sense in many contemporary reviews that fantasy is not something to be over-indulged and should possibly be avoided altogether. The *Variety* review of *The Wizard of Oz* concluded that although 'there's an audience for "Oz" wherever there's a projection machine and a screen ... fantasies and fairy stories are way out of the groove of run-of-the-mill film entertainment' (Anon. 1939b) and the same publication's review of *Arabian Nights* (1942) noted that 'although there's a tinge of fantasy, producer Walter Wanger wisely steers away from the magic of fabled times to concentrate attention on lusty action and romance' bringing the film 'in tune with present audience requirements' (Anon. 1942). The review does not elaborate upon what the requirements of a wartime

American audience might be but fantasy, it seems, was not considered appropriate. By 1955, the *Variety* review of *The Glass Slipper* suggested that this 'whimsical treatment of the Cinderella fairy tale' should appeal to those who 'prefer to go outside regular types of screenfare for their film entertainment' but that 'fantasy does not have the kind of popular appeal that will make the general theatre patron lay his cash down at the wickets' (Anon. 1955).

One of the consequences of this downplaying of the presence of fantasy in film has been its marginalisation, rather than the acknowledgement that fantasy is a natural and common instinct expressed by many films and filmmakers. Fantasy is far more active in film than the official industry statistics suggest. If we consider the UK Film Council's Research and Statistic Unit's (RSU) annual audit of films released in the UK, the figures relating to fantasy can result in some skewed conclusions about its presence in contemporary cinema. The RSU allocates up to five categories of genre to each film released in the UK, with the 2004–06 spreadsheets listing a film's primary genre only.[4] To take the 2006 audit as a sample, six films were listed as having fantasy as their primary genre (*Ju-On: The Grudge 2* (2003), *Mirrormask* (2005), *Zathura* (2005), *Lady in the Water* (2006), *Pan's Labyrinth* and *Eragon*) compared with twelve for romance, 24 for horror, 24 for thriller, forty for documentary, 122 for comedy and 153 for drama. Taking into account a certain degree of subjectivity over determining which genre is considered to be the dominant in any particular film (both *Tideland* and *Superman Returns* (2006) have strong fantasy elements but appear in the lists for drama and action respectively), fantasy would appear to be far from a major force in contemporary cinema based solely on the number of films released in a given year. Yet fantasy often punches above its weight. In 2005, following the RSU's figures given in the corresponding statistical yearbook, fantasy only accounted for a mere 0.9% of all films released that year according to genre – four films deemed by the RSU to be principally fantasy in contrast to 181 films classified as drama. But those four fantasy films generated double the amount of box-office revenue (£132.1 million) garnered by the same year's entire output of drama films (£65.8 million). This reversal in fortunes at the box office was due to the four titles being heavily promoted, receiving a wide release and benefiting from being either part of a major ongoing franchise (*Harry Potter and the Goblet of Fire*), an adaptation of a popular book with cross-generational appeal

(*Harry Potter* again, *Charlie and the Chocolate Factory*, *The Chronicles of Narnia: The Lion, the Witch and the Wardrobe*) or having a charismatic star and director with a distinctive style (Johnny Depp and Tim Burton in the case of *Charlie and the Chocolate Factory*, Heath Ledger and Terry Gilliam for *The Brothers Grimm*).

Taken as a whole, the RSU figures suggest a minimal presence of fantasy in contemporary cinema released in the UK over the 2003–07 period: six films in 2006–07, four films in 2005–06, five films in 2004–05 and five films in 2003–04. A more accurate figure for fantasy can be generated for 2003–04 where up to five genres are listed for each film released rather than the perceived generic dominant – in this instance the number of fantasy films increases from five to 24. Yet even here, the list erases fantasy from films where it is very much present and a crucial aspect of the film's narrative (such as *Big Fish* and *The Singing Detective* (both 2003)). The most telling example from the 2003–04 list is *Lilja 4-ever* (2002), Lukas Moodysson's harrowing tale about a 16-year-old girl (Lilja, played by Oksana Akinshina) from 'somewhere in the former Soviet Union' who is abandoned by her mother and then betrayed into the sex industry. The RSU list allocates the film only one genre category – drama – and for almost the entire duration of the film this proves to be correct. There is not much respite from the bleakness of Lilja's life, apart from moments of friendship shared with a younger boy, Volodya (Artiom Bogucharskij), another outcast. Volodya commits suicide and Lilja falls into prostitution before moving to Sweden, thinking she is going to be joined by her new 'boyfriend' only to be imprisoned in an apartment as a sex slave. With disturbing point-of-view shots from Lilja's perspective of a series of clients forcing themselves on her, we are shown that there seems to be no way out for Lilja. Just when the film appears to be cutting off all possibility of hope from Lilja, however, Moodysson introduces an element of fantasy that jars with what has hitherto been an unremittingly grim drama. Battered and unconscious, Lilja is awoken by Volodya, now sporting a pair of somewhat awkward-looking white wings attached to his back. The assumption is that Volodya's appearance, returned from the dead, is a product of Lilja's dreaming or imagination. Volodya informs Lilja that the door to the apartment in which she has been imprisoned is now open and she can escape. Alone in an alien country, Lilja goes on the run before throwing herself from a motorway bridge, despite the winged-Volodya's plea for her not to jump.

The film ends with Lilja, happy at last, playing catch with Volodya on top of a run-down building, surrounded by wire, both now wearing an identical pair of white wings.

How do we make sense of this ending? Tony Rayns (2003) has described the appearance of the winged Volodya as a 'staggering aesthetic miscalculation' lurching the film into 'sentimental nonsense'. The wings do not convince – they move stiffly and appear to be straight out of a school nativity play – but that, perhaps, is the point. Earlier in the film, we have learnt that Lilja's dearest possession is a painting of an angel and a child. The wings grown by Volodya and Lilja seem to be modelled on those in the painting – Lilja draws on the limited sources available to her in order to dream of something else. If the closing sequence is Lilja's dying fantasy then it serves to underline the poverty of her imagination and, in its naïve manifestation, is a poignant evocation of the deprivation Lilja has endured. There is no dazzling Hollywood CGI here or shafts of golden light and a magical court as in Ofelia's dying fantasy at the end of *Pan's Labyrinth*. The best Lilja can imagine Heaven to be is a crumbling rooftop, running and playing basketball with her only friend in life and a pair of cheap wings as markers of their angelic status. Rather than being sentimental nonsense, Moodysson provides a final comment on the abuse of children and the erosion of innocence, juxtaposing bleak reality with a child's fantasy as a reminder that, for all her appalling experiences, Lilja was a girl stripped of her childhood. The ending is not unlike that of Andrei Tarkovsky's debut feature *Ivanovo detstvo* (*Ivan's Childhood*, 1962). Like Lilja, Ivan (Nikolai Burlaev) has experience beyond his years – although only twelve, he is a scout in the Russian army, obsessed with avenging the murder of his family by the Nazis. As with *Lilja 4-ever*, the final discovery that Ivan is dead, executed by the Nazis, is followed immediately by his dream of a better, innocent world, running

Final fantasy in *Lilja 4-ever* (2002)

along a beach with his lost childhood friend, into the blackness of the film's end. The gulf between Ivan and Lilja's fantasies and the reality of their existence emphasises what they have been denied, the absence of love and hope from their lives. Fantasy, then, is a key tool employed by Moodysson, even if only in the film's closing moments. Consequently, the omission of fantasy from those films in the RSU lists, such as *Lilja 4-ever*, in which it is present but not used extensively, furthers the impression that fantasy is a specific type of film rather than something that can be mobilised by filmmakers in even the harshest and most naturalistic of narratives, across a wide variety of genres.

Fantasy as impulse – Méliès the magician

This notion of fantasy, limiting it to a specific set of semantic features, is an industry construct and, in this respect, the film industry has followed in the footsteps of its counterpart in publishing. As David Hartwell observes, 'the fantasy category is a new thing, invented by a publishing industry and made a success as a marketing category only as recently as the 1970s' (1999: 1). Fantasy for the contemporary film industry has tended to crystallise around a combination of Tolkien/Conan/Harry Potter/Dungeons & Dragons sword and sorcery but, as we have established, that is only a small aspect of fantasy's range. Instead of a genre or a mode, I would agree with Kathryn Hume that we should think of fantasy as an *impulse*. For Hume, fantasy and mimesis are the two basic impulses in literature with fantasy being the 'desire to change givens and alter reality – out of boredom, play, vision, longing for something lacking, or need for metaphoric images' (1984: 20). Fantasy in this sense establishes itself as a natural activity rather than a niche genre and we should not, as Hume states, need to 'claim a work as a fantasy any more than we identify a work as a mimesis' (ibid.). This notion of two core impulses in literature, fantasy and mimesis, is in keeping with much of the writing on early film history, which conventionally identifies, as Siegfried Kracauer put it, 'two main tendencies', expressed in the contrasting approaches in the late nineteenth and early twentieth century of the 'strict realist' Lumière brothers and Georges Méliès, 'who gave free rein to his artistic imagination' (1999: 173). Discussing this 'conceptual neatness' of film history, Robert B. Ray refers to Jean-Luc Godard's observation that although 'cinema is spectacle – Méliès – and research – Lumière', the

41

two do not have to be in opposition: 'I have always wanted to do research in the form of a spectacle' (Godard quoted in Ray 2001: 3).

If the Lumière brothers, Auguste and Louis, were the first to establish cinema as a collective, social experience following the screening of their 'actualités' at Paris's Grand Café in late 1895, then it was the conjurer Georges Méliès who first explored at length the fantasy impulse in cinema. For Hans Richter, Méliès was 'the father of the fantastic film' and 'the first to unlock the secret powers of the camera' (1986: 53) in films such as *Le Manoir du diable* (*The Haunted Castle*, 1896), *La Caverne maudite* (*The Cave of the Demons*, 1898), *Barbe-bleue* (*Blue-beard*, 1901) and, most famously, *Le Voyage dans la lune* (*A Trip to the Moon*, 1902). Méliès was active as a filmmaker until 1912 when his approach to narrative style and film form began to appear increasingly dated when contrasted with the more dynamic narratives of filmmakers such as D. W. Griffith. Méliès was less interested in film as a medium through which to tell stories and more as a showcase for a sequence of wild and wonderful tricks – but the impulse for cinematic fantasy had been primed and set. In doing so, film was only expressing an impulse that has been active in human societies for thousands of years. In his foreword to André Bazin's *What is Cinema?*, Dudley Andrew notes Bazin's essay on the children's film in which the genre is treated as a 'constant human impulse: people of all eras and cultures have entertained children with fabulous tales' (2004: xviii). That impulse is not just the province of children's tales – rather than being contained to one genre and demographic, it runs in and out of registers, genres and age ranges. As Mobina Hashmi, Bill Kirkpatrick and Billy Vermillion propose, 'we might be better served by understanding science fiction and fantasy as a certain perspective toward present social, cultural, and economic realities, an orientation that can cross discourses and genres' (2003: 1). In the next chapter, we will consider some of the genres in which the fantasy impulse has been most evident.

2   TYPES OF FANTASY: ANGELS, GENIES, SWORDS AND SORCERERS

Although the last chapter argued that fantasy is an impulse rather than a single coherent genre, there are, of course, a number of genres and sub-genres in which the fantasy impulse is pushed to the fore. It is a range that continues to expand as new types and trends appear. When Hans Richter was writing *The Struggle for the Film* in the late 1930s, he identified just three main types of film: fiction, documentary and fantastic. For Richter, the fantastic film (whose function was to confound, distort and change reality, 'allowing the impossible and the nonsensical to become visible' (1986: 53)), having stemmed from Georges Méliès and 'ceased to exist' in the 'classic period' of the silent cinema following World War One (1986: 56), had now expanded to include the avant-garde of filmmakers such as René Clair as well as Walt Disney and Charlie Chaplin. Richter's range is narrow (there is no place for the likes of Kong or Fairbanks' Thief) but any list of types of fantasy film compiled today would have to be far more expansive. Kenneth Von Gunden's 1989 overview of 'the great fantasy films' benefits from a further fifty years of fantasy cinema to draw on, by which time several types had begun to proliferate in contrast to Richter's era. Von Gunden includes in his pantheon an example of the fairy tale film (*La Belle et la bête (Beauty and the Beast*, 1946)), sword and sorcery (*Conan the Barbarian*), child's fantasy (*The 5,000 Fingers of Dr T*), the guardian angel (*It's a Wonderful Life*), ancient mythology (*Jason and the Argonauts* (1963)), the giant monster film (*King Kong*), the hidden paradise (*Lost Horizon* (1937)), the superhero film

(*Superman* (1978)), the *Arabian Nights* film (*The Thief of Bagdad* (1940)), the child as hero (*Time Bandits*), the ghost film (*Topper* (1937)) and the fabulous journey (*The Wizard of Oz*). The boundaries marking out these genres are not firmly defined by Von Gunden or provided with much semantic and syntactic depth, leaving plenty of scope for overlap: 'child's fantasy' and 'child as hero' could just as easily apply to *The Wizard of Oz*, and 'the fabulous journey' could include both *Time Bandits* and *Jason and the Argonauts* as well as *King Kong*. Some of Von Gunden's categories are hazy – 'other worlds, other times', although referring to *The Dark Crystal* could, again, be applied to several of Von Gunden's case studies and does not provide the basis for a coherent genre. There is also an emphasis on juvenilia, which is perhaps understandable given Von Gunden's introductory note that fantasy films 'activate the child that still resides in all of us' (1989: viii). If the genre of 'child's fantasy' is foregrounded then one could add a related category of 'adult's fantasy' with appropriate examples being *Billy Liar* (1963) or *Juliet of the Spirits*, both featuring central adult characters whose fantasies are represented within the film.

Unlike Von Gunden, Alec Worley's 2005 critical survey of fantasy cinema operates from a more manageable range of sub-genres, namely, the fairy tale film, 'earthbound fantasy' meaning those films set in our known world, which is then disrupted by a fantastic element (such as *It's a Wonderful Life*, *Freaky Friday* (1976), *Die Blechtrommel* (*The Tin Drum*, 1978) and *Being John Malkovich* (1999)), heroic fantasy and, lastly, epic fantasy, which Worley distinguishes from heroic fantasy through the epic variant's scope ('putting life into the grandest perspective') and tone ('epic fantasies [cannot] use irony to distance themselves from their own histrionics … these movies demand total commitment to their premise' (2005: 233)). As with Von Gunden, there is still potential for overlap between these categories – *The Fisher King*, for example, takes place on our known world in early 1990s New York and so might be considered an 'earthbound fantasy' but it also draws directly on Arthurian romance, specifically Grail mythology and the principle of the heroic quest, connecting it to other categories from Worley's survey. There is nothing unusual about this blending of genres – as Janet Staiger has discussed in her interrogation of the 'genre purity hypothesis' (1997: 14), Hollywood films have mixed genres since the classical era of productions such as *Casablanca* (1942), described in its promotional material as having adventure, romance, comedy, melodrama, 'anti-Axis propaganda', action and suspense (ibid.). *The Lord of the Rings* is, variously, an epic fantasy, a sword and sorcery film, an action/adventure film, a war film and a road movie (to pick out some of the most prominent genres at play in the trilogy), a necessary fusion perhaps, given the franchise's financial need to appeal to a wide demographic. This book cannot, therefore, hope to detail in depth all the types and sub-genres of fantasy film that have emerged over the last hundred years, and so the remainder of the chapter will only focus on some of the most prominent.

The 'film blanc' or supernatural rom-com

Categories come and go, as a result of both critical and industrial fashion. If 'other worlds, other times' has not taken root neither, for example, has Paul Valenti's proposal, in 1978, of the *'film blanc'* as a variety of fantasy that flourished briefly in Hollywood during World War Two. This context is key to the *film blanc*. The first examples of *film blanc* began to appear at the same time as the emergence of *film noir*. *Film noir* was a critical term developed by French critics in the late 1940s and early 1950s, with the suggestion that *noir*'s characteristic alienation, urban malaise and portrayal of inescapable fate responded to a specific set of socio-historical circumstances (such as postwar anxiety and the fear, as Reid and Walker note, that the spectre of the economic Depression might return (see 1993: 65)). Valenti argues that the *film blanc* provided the antidote to the very same anxieties that fuelled *film noir*, offering 'redemption from this dark vale of soul-making and the opportunity to show that man is deserving of something more than the grim lot assigned by fortune' (1978: 303). These particular fantasy films would include titles such as *Beyond Tomorrow* (1940), *Between Two Worlds* (1944), *It's a Wonderful Life* and *A Matter of Life and Death* (a British film but one received enthusiastically in the US, under the title *Stairway to Heaven*), with shared characteristics being a 'mortal's death or lapse into a dream', the intervention of a benevolent agent from 'the world beyond' (such as Clarence the angel in *It's a Wonderful Life* or Conductor 71 in *A Matter of Life and Death*), a strong romance plot and the ultimate escape from the spirit world to return to a mortal existence (Valenti 1978: 274).

That the *film blanc* has not become established as a genre category is less a reflection of the validity of Valenti's work – Martin Norden (1982) identifies a similar body of films in his brief study of US fantasy cinema from

1945–51. Several factors, however, have prevented Valenti's term from gaining widespread use. Firstly, Valenti was writing thirty years after the event, whereas the initial *noir* critics were only a handful of years behind the first wave of *noir* films and were active when *film noir* was still being regularly produced. Secondly, the lack of critical attention given to fantasy in general would make it difficult for the *film blanc* to take root as an accepted concept in film studies. More pragmatically, there is the somewhat short-lived nature of the actual genre. For Valenti, the *film blanc* declined in output after 1947, due, he suggests, to it being at odds with the 'pessimism and realism of much postwar film' (1978: 302). Valenti's suggestion is somewhat simplistic and does not account for the postwar success of lighter genres such as comedy and the musical: following the same logic, one might expect these to be a victim of the same pessimism. As Steve Neale observes, the rush to explain the existence of *film noir* (or, conversely in this case, the decline of the *film blanc*) and relate it to a particular historical moment has often glossed over a more complex context and set of causal factors than convenient, albeit genuine, fears of Communism and nuclear devastation. As Neale has noted, 'Hollywood was making cheerful and optimistic films like *Road to Utopia* [1944], *The Bells of St Mary's* [1945], *The Egg and I* [1947] and *The Bachelor and the Bobbysoxer* [1947] at the same time as it was making angst-ridden thrillers, and by and large these were the biggest successes at the box office' (2000: 158). The *film blanc* may well have declined following its peak during the 1940s but it has not totally disappeared, with latter-day descendants of the genre including films such as *Bruce Almighty* (2003).

A notable box-office success on its initial release in the US, *Bruce Almighty* corresponds to Valenti's criteria for the *film blanc* genre. Bruce (Jim Carrey) is unhappy in life and complains to God (Morgan Freeman), the ultimate example of Valenti's 'benevolent agent'. He is given access to God's powers but abuses them for his own personal gain before coming to realise his selfishness and failings as a human being. Distraught at the effect of his behaviour on his girlfriend, Grace (Jennifer Aniston), Bruce is killed in a road accident but God allows him to return to his mortal existence when Bruce reveals that the one thing he wants is for Grace to find a man that will make her happy. Bruce comes back to life a changed man and is reunited with Grace. There is much here that is familiar to films such as *It's a Wonderful Life* but *Bruce Almighty* raises interesting questions in terms of the context of its production and reception and the dangers of a straightforward 'reflectionist' model as a means of interpreting a film's relationship to its socio-historical context. If Valenti argued that the perceived pessimism of the postwar years in the US proved hostile to the sentimental optimism of the *film blanc* genre, how do we account for the major box-office success of *Bruce Almighty*, released into an America still coming to terms with the devastating attacks of 9/11, now fully engaged in a 'War on Terror' and two months into a military campaign in Iraq (having achieved its initial stated objective of toppling the regime of Saddam Hussein)?

Bruce *Almighty* opened over the Memorial Day weekend, a national holiday commemorating those US citizens who have died in military conflict. The film's fusion of comedy and fantasy might appear to have been at odds with this climate of fear and sombre reflection. Yet, despite predictions that it would lose out to the science fiction action blockbuster *The Matrix Reloaded* (2003), *Bruce Almighty* gained one of the largest opening box-office audiences ever recorded in the Memorial Day weekend slot. Writing for *Box Office Mojo*, Brandon Gray (2003) suggested that the film's success was precisely due to the cultural climate being 'in such a mood for laughs that it's truly been the year of comedy' and that the film also had a 'universal "What If?" premise' ('If you could be God for one week, what would you do?' ran the tagline). But as well as being a vehicle for a popular star (the film proved to be a return to box-office form for Carrey) and a comedy in which Bruce is able to make his (selfish) fantasies come true (such as enlarging his girlfriend's breasts and gaining revenge on a deceitful work colleague), *Bruce Almighty* also provides, however limited and indirectly, a discussion around what C. S. Lewis, writing in 1940, termed 'the problem of pain' (see 1977). How can a world in which appalling acts take place, such as the destruction of the World Trade Center on 11 September 2001 or the degradation of an entire country's society and infrastructure, as happened to Iraq in the wake of the US-led coalition's strikes and occupation, be compatible with the concept of an omnipotent and benevolent, loving God? *Bruce Almighty*, not surprisingly, does not refer to these specific examples but it does provide a response to dealing with the problem of pain. In a pivotal scene, Bruce and God discuss the nature of miracles and the importance of individual responsibility as opposed to a reliance on God's intervention:

> Parting your soup is not a miracle, Bruce, it's a magic trick. A single
> mom who's working two jobs and still finds time to take her kids to

soccer practice, that's a miracle. A teenager who says no to drugs and yes to an education, that's a miracle. People want me to do everything for them, and what they don't realise is – they have the power. You want to see a miracle, son? Be the miracle.

If the film does not fall back here on a facile fantasy that all will be well with a wave of an omnipotent hand, elsewhere it expresses the dilemma facing any omnipresent divine being: how to respond to an eternal stream of millions upon millions of often conflicting prayers. God is absolved of any blame and responsibility – the responsibility is humanity's and God is established as a wise guide that mankind does not pay enough heed to. All of which might seem to place the film on course for a conclusion that is in line with the discussion of individual responsibility, facing the consequences of one's actions and the portrayal of God as benevolent observer rather than active intervener in human affairs. Yet God's decision at the end of the film, to resurrect Bruce and allow him to return to Grace, completely undermines the film's central message and its brief engagement with the problem of pain, calling into question the motives behind God's behaviour and decision-making process – who lives, who dies and why? Why is Bruce deemed worthy of being saved and not the millions of others throughout human history? *Bruce Almighty* is pulled in two opposing directions. It complicates one naïve fantasy only to surrender to the dream of another: that true love and the monogamous heterosexual relationship will triumph over death (Bruce's wish that Grace find a man who can make her happy is only achievable through his resurrection rather than the possibility that, in time, she might meet someone else). We may live in fearful times but *Bruce Almighty* suggests that, whether one describes it as a *film blanc* or supernatural comedy/romance, this genre does not simply disappear when the going gets tough.

The fairy tale film

When we think of fairy tales we might conjure up notions of pure storytelling and childhood innocence – but fairy tales are far from innocent. Fairy tales are big business. As Jack Zipes surmises, 'it is not by chance that the fairy tale film has become the most popular cultural commodity in America, if not the world' (1997: 1). Zipes is one of the most prolific writers on fairy tales (key figures also include Vladimir Propp, Bruno Bettelheim and Marina Warner) and, in identifying the fairy tale film as the most prevalent cultural commodity of the late twentieth century, Zipes refers to a wide range of films from *The Never Ending Story* (1984) to *The Lion King* (1994), *Splash* (1984) and *The Princess Bride* (1987), or video re-releases like *Snow White and the Seven Dwarfs* (1937) and *Pinocchio* (1940). The clothes and settings may get updated, as they are in *Pretty Woman* (1990), where the Fairy Godmother's magic wand is replaced by businessman's credit card so that Vivian the hooker (Julia Roberts) can go to the ball (or polo match), but the same basic source material (in this case 'Cinderella') is still being mined. Yet the fairy tale film goes back much further than any of these titles and can be traced back to the origins of cinema. Méliès was making fairy tale films as early as 1897 with *La Cigale et la fourmi* from Aesop's fable 'The Grasshopper and the Ant'. More recognisable were the three films Méliès made based on the tales of Charles Perrault: *Cendrillon* (1899), *Le Petit chaperon rouge* (1901) and *Barbe-bleue* or *Cinderella*, *Little Red Riding Hood* and *Blue Beard* to give them their English titles. If the fairy tale film spans the full reach of film history then, similarly, it has not just been confined to Hollywood and the West. There are rich traditions of fairy tale cinema outside of the Disney animation studios, particularly in Eastern Europe with Alexander Ptushko and Aleksandr Rou in the former Soviet Union or Václav Vorlícek in the Czech Republic being among the most prominent.

It is no surprise, though, that the name of Walt Disney looms large in the brief list above. It is the work of Disney from the late 1930s onwards that, Zipes argues, 'set the model for most of the animated fairy tale films that were to be produced in the later twentieth century' (1997: 71). This model is also ideological, perpetuating those values and beliefs endorsed by Disney, not least, Zipes asserts, in relation to 'clear-cut gender roles that associated women with domesticity and men with action and power' (ibid.). Fairy tales have always done this – the first collections of fairy tales produced in Europe (in France and Italy in the sixteenth and seventeenth centuries) also sought to address the concerns and interests of the privileged sections of society doing the tale-telling. These initial collections of fairy tales, such as Giambattista Basile's *Il Pentamerone* (1634–36) or the *contes des fées* (tales of the fairies), which flourished among the (mainly female) French salon writers, Marie-Catherine D'Aulnoy being the most prominent, tended to be told by adults to adults. It was not until 1756 that Madame Le Prince de Beaumont would publish a version of *Beauty and the Beast*: the first known example of a fairy tale specifically targeted at children. Later collections (such as Hans Christian Andersen's *Fairy Tales Told For Children* (1835)) would be aimed at children, unlike the originals.

Historically, fairy tales have been understood as the product of a literary culture rather than the predominantly oral mode of delivery of folk tales. Fairy tales became increasingly institutionalised and were often a mass-produced version of an earlier folk tale. It is all too easy to split fairy tales and folk tales into a straightforward literary culture versus oral culture dualism. As Alan Dundes (1965) cautions, however, some official cultures are purely oral and, equally, some forms of folk culture (book marginalia, epitaphs and traditional letters such as chain letters or e-mails spread via distribution lists and block posting) are transmitted in a written form or via neither oral nor literary means (such as folk dances, gestures and games). If folk tales are not static in form, tending to be flexible and changing in accordance with the tale-teller and the situation in which they are telling the tale, fairy tales tend to be much more fixed and controlled once they are written down. With the initial literary fairy tales, the audience was limited by education and economics: illiteracy was high and books were a luxury few could afford. Not surprisingly, it was the privileged classes who could most readily access these tales, which were augmented to express the values of this demographic. During the nineteenth century, folk tales were increasingly transformed into fairy tales made safe for consumption by children. The folk tales collected by the Brothers Grimm in 1812, for example, were altered so that they supported Victorian ideals. As Zipes claims, folk tales were 'rewritten and made into didactic fairy tales for children so that they would not be harmed by the violence, crudity and fantastic exaggeration of the originals' (2002: 18). In effect, the development of the fairy tale is an example of what Theodor Adorno and Max Horkheimer (2002) termed standardisation – the process by which the culture industry of capitalist societies streamlines cultural products so that any aspects that might challenge the values of that society are ironed out or justified as aberrations. It is not too much of a leap then to go from the mass-produced fairy tale books of the nineteenth century to the even more pervasively mass-produced fairy tale films of the twentieth century. The dominant figure here, of course, is Disney.

Disney's first animated experiments, across 1922 and 1923, were fairy tales (including *Puss in Boots*, *Jack and the Beanstalk* and *Little Red Riding Hood*) as was his first animated feature film, *Snow White and the Seven Dwarfs*, followed by a second animated fairy tale feature, *Pinocchio*. Disney interpretations of fairy tales have tended not to be discussed in favourable terms by academic studies. Jack Zipes has offered a sustained political critique of Disney's output (taking in the studio's classical era and those films produced by the company following Walt Disney's death in 1966) and the films have received similar stern criticism in feminist analyses for their regressive portrayal of female characters (see, for example, Wasko 2001: 132–6). Although this criticism should not be negated, the artistic achievement of Disney, not just in the field of the animated fairy tale, can often become lost. Disney himself received an astonishing 59 Academy Award nominations over the course of his career, winning on 22 occasions (with four further honorary and special awards). The aesthetic charm and brilliance of much of Disney's output (taking into account kitsch misfires such as the Pastoral Symphony sequence in *Fantasia* (1940)), not least in relation to the synchronisation of sound and image, has delighted and impressed millions, including prominent filmmakers such as Sergei Eisenstein and Michael Powell (Disney's influence on Powell is clear in *The Red Shoes* (1948) and *The Tales of Hoffmann* (1951) but it is also evident in brief moments such as the opening to *A Matter of Life and Death*, whose initial journey across the galaxy, gradually homing in on Earth, recalls the similar journey through space that opens 'The Rite of Spring' episode in *Fantasia*).

Nonetheless, admiration for the films' formal qualities and technical skill should not displace any analysis of their content and often pernicious subtext. Zipes is foremost here, and in a chapter titled 'Breaking the Disney Spell', he outlines the celebration of the male hero, which takes place at the expense of the central female character, even in those tales where the male hero is not the principal figure:

It may seem strange to argue that Disney perpetuated a male myth through his fairy tale films when, with the exception of *Pinocchio*, they all featured young women as 'heroines'. However, despite their beauty and charm, Sleeping Beauty, Cinderella, and the other heroines are pale and pathetic compared to the more active and demonic characters in the film. The witches are not only agents of evil but represent erotic and subversive forces that are more appealing for the artists who drew them and for the audiences. The young women are like helpless ornaments in need of protection, and when it comes to the action of the film, they are omitted. (1994: 90)

The clearest example of this tendency in Disney would be the first of these films, *Snow White and the Seven Dwarfs*, which gives far more prominence to the Prince's role than the Brothers Grimm do in their account. Poisoned by the wicked witch-queen, in Disney it is the Prince who awakens Snow White with a kiss. But in the Grimms' version she wakes up when one of the dwarfs carrying her glass coffin stumbles. Disney sanitises the tale – the witch does not suffer the punishment meted out to her by the Grimms (forced to dance in red-hot iron shoes) and it is difficult to imagine Disney's dwarfs (Grumpy apart) behaving like the gang of time-travelling crooks in Terry Gilliam's *Time Bandits*. The Grimms' tales are frequently clear about the domesticated role for women but in classic Disney there is a glorification of the male hero often to the detriment of the main female character's agency. Janet Wasko notes Kay Stone's 1975 observation that 'while the Grimms' heroines are relatively uninspiring, "those of Walt Disney seem barely alive. In fact, two of them hardly manage to stay awake"' (2001: 133). The result of this approach to the portrayal of female characters is an extremely narrow and clichéd set of characteristics for children to identify with and learn from. In their cross-cultural study of how children incorporate mass-media fantasies into their own 'make-believe' worlds and creative play, Maya Götz, Dafna Lemish, Amy Aidman and Hyesung Moon discovered that girls 'use creative strategies to adapt and incorporate female heroines from the slim selection provided through media offerings' (2005: 133) with such strategies including the incorporation of fewer media references, ignoring the male heroes altogether and inventing their own characters. Films such as *Shrek* (2001) offer a rare alternative to the majority of media texts, which, Götz *et al.* note, 'promote restrictive ideologies of femininity, glorify heterosexual romance as a central goal for girls, encourage male domination in relationships, and stress the importance of beautification through consumption ... dismissing the validity of their own sexual feelings and desires apart from masculine desire' (2005: 148). The princess figure is the most obvious character through which these themes are expressed in the fairy tale films produced by Disney.

'Any girl can do that': Popelka shows the Prince how to shoot in *Three Hazelnuts for Cinderella* (1973)

Other approaches to the fairy tale film, outside the dominant Disney model, have provided more diverse, active and empowered heroines. Václav Vorlícek's *Tri orísky pro Popelku* (*Three Hazelnuts for Cinderella*, 1973) is a much-loved favourite in the Czech Republic and a Christmas ritual in several countries. It features a crossbow-shooting Cinderella, or Popelka (Libuse Safránková) in the original Czech, who does not swoon and sing at the first sight of the Prince but must be pursued and won, having sabotaged the Prince's hunting trip, insulted him and then beaten him in a crossbow contest. In this film, Popelka/Cinderella has a diversity of roles – she is a menial worker and huntress *as well as* a princess – and, in order to win her hand in marriage, the Prince must acknowledge all aspects of her life. From the same era, Jacques Demy's *Peau d'âne* (*Donkey Skin*, 1970) channels both Disney (through its use of vivid colour and song, via a score by Michel Legrand) and Jean Cocteau's seminal fairy tale film *La belle et la bête* (Cocteau is referenced through the use of reverse motion, living statues and, most obviously, the casting of Jean Marais, Cocteau's former partner and the Beast in *La belle et la bête*, as the King). With her opulent dresses, Catherine Deneuve's

Princess may seem to typify the trope of 'beautification through consumption' but, as Marina Warner (1993a: 31) has suggested, the film offers a sly critique of patriarchal authority and Oedipal fantasy theory. The actual tale of *Donkey Skin* contains enough elements to make it unacceptable to the more sanitised and conservative ethos of Disney – the titular donkey excretes gold and jewels, the King is compelled to marry his own daughter, she then goes into exile wearing the hide of the magic donkey in order to avoid marrying her father. However, although the film does not censor this material, neither does Demy dwell on the story's inherent horror and grotesque aspects, coating the film instead with a camp aesthetic to sugar its troubling themes but leave them present all the same. This sweetening of the story's tone serves to highlight the 'covering up' of these themes (the sex, violence, incest, grotesquerie and so on of the original versions) and their omission from the majority of institutionalised fairy tales – Demy's surface gloss draws attention to the censorship and denial at work elsewhere in other interpretations. For Warner, this stylised approach enables Demy to 'dramatise the daughter's rejection of her father, rather than her fantasy of love for the father which is how the fairy tale *Donkey Skin* is usually interpreted in psychoanalytical material – that is to say, it is presented as a transferred fantasy, and a desiring daughter imagines that her father is in love with her' (ibid.).

If *Peau d'âne* plays with the adult themes embedded in its tale then Jaromíl Jireš' *Valerie a týden divů* (*Valerie and Her Week of Wonders*, 1970) fully embraces the possibilities of the adult fairy tale film. Based on a 1935 fairy tale by the avant-garde writer Vítězslav Nezval, *Valerie and Her Week of Wonders* is another example of the impressive tradition of fantasy filmmaking in Czech cinema. The film's striking audio-visual style makes extensive use of montage and its non-linearity ensures that, in formal terms alone, it is a far from mainstream film. As a tale about the sexual awakening of its central character (played by Jaroslava Schallerová) and, like other adult fairy tales such as *Pan's Labyrinth*, a critique of the older generation and its abuse of youth, *Valerie and Her Week of Wonders* does not attempt to moralise about sex or simplify its portrayal for polite consumption. In Jireš' film, as David Melville (2007) identifies, socio-political control is equated with vampirism and 'an aged elite prolongs its youth and power by feasting on the beautiful, innocent young'. Tanya Krzywinska (2003) notes that 'the film constructs adult sexuality as strange, mysterious and enigmatic: the people we think we as children know so well turn out to have dark, bestial desires that undermine our earlier idealisation of them'. Yet this approach to sex is not employed to terrify Valerie and deter her from exploring her own sexuality. As Krzywinska observes, 'like the heroines of pre-sanitised fairytales, [Valerie] faces all the mysteries that come her way boldly and with wide-eyed curiosity'. Not surprisingly, this portrayal of a more empowered fairy tale heroine would be an influence on the British writer Angela Carter and would inform the 1984 film based on her revisionist fairy tales, *The Company of Wolves*.

Directed by Neil Jordan and with a screenplay by Jordan and Carter, the film develops the latter's short story of the same name contained in her 1979 collection, *The Bloody Chamber*, as well as incorporating several other of her short stories. *The Company of Wolves* reworks the story of 'Little Red Riding Hood', giving it a sensuousness missing from most versions of the tale from the Victorian era onwards. Where earlier takes on the story, following Perrault's moralistic interpretation, functioned as a warning to girls on the threshold of puberty about the perils of spending time with 'wolfish' men, in Carter's re-imagining the girl (Rosaleen (Sarah Patterson) in the film) tames the wolf-man and embraces her budding sexuality.

The film contains a variety of approaches to the supernatural. Some of the transformation scenes from human to wolf are done with simple trickery, others are dwelt on as loud and unpleasant animatronics – and these scenes take the film away from the fairy tale genre and more towards horror. They find their origin, however, as Charlotte Crofts notes (see 2003:

Enigmatic symbols at the top of the tree: *The Company of Wolves* (1984)

112), in the 1980 radio play of the story, which describes the shape-shifting in detail through words (unlike the short story). This detailed metamorphosis on radio is then transposed visually to film as an explicit transformation (in the story it takes place in the twinkling of a sentence). For Maggie Anwell, these violent transformations in the film were so memorable they undermined Carter's attempts to celebrate female sexuality: as Crofts summarises Anwell's reading, 'the werewolf transformations are inherently connected to aggressive, masculine sexuality – reinscribing the patriarchal power structures of the original fairy tale, rather than subverting them as in Carter's original story' (2003: 111). But, as Crofts argues, the film's graphic transformations are largely contained in the stories being told by Granny (Angela Lansbury) – stories that are *meant* to scare Rosaleen about men (as in Perrault's version) and outside of Granny's tales the transformations are less troubling to Rosaleen.

The Company of Wolves is a much more complex (and, for some, confused) film than a straightforward inversion of the Disney model. Its use of symbolism leaves it open to interpretation and many possible readings. Similarly, the film's ultimate stance on female fantasy and desire is enigmatic. One of the most memorable scenes in the film is Rosaleen's climbing of the great tree, seemingly at the heart of the forest. With glorious music swelling triumphantly in George Fenton's score, here evocative of Ravel (himself no stranger to using myths and fairy tales as source material for his music), Rosaleen finally rises above the forest that her Granny has used to warn and terrify her – and in doing so finds what? Space to grow free from authority and repression? At the top of the tree is a stork's nest, containing four eggs, a hand mirror and a pot of lipstick. Rosaleen applies the lipstick and admires her new look in the mirror – as she does so the four eggs crack open to reveal small baby figurines. What does it all mean?

Carole Zucker suggests that the tree-climbing sequence represents Rosaleen's entry into womanhood:

> The sequence is laden with significance, but perhaps most unmistakable, and most important is the resemblance to the tree of knowledge. There are the archetypal images of loss, innocence, and entry into the world of experience ... a movement away from the ordered, protected existence of the parental home, as well as from the safety

of 'the path'. It is a point of no return, for ... Rosaleen is neither girl nor woman. Rosaleen's lipstick is likened to the blood on the wolf's mouth, yet the wolf poses no apparent danger for the young girl. While a tear is shed for her loss of childhood, Rosaleen's entrance into the erotic – the emergence of appetite (she, like the wolf, can be a predator; she wants the giant phallus, not a mere lad), the masturbatory stroking of her lips with moist fingers, the spectre of childbirth, her mother's natural acceptance of her daughter's *rite de passage*, do not provoke – in the context of the dream world – fear or anxiety. The menstrual imagery of the tree scene – Rosaleen's red lipstick – is also typical of the references to 'first blood' found in so many fairytales. (2000: 68)

This may well be true – at least until one hears Jordan's DVD commentary about the same scene's perceived symbolism. Discussing how he and Carter came up with the contents of the eggs in the stork's nest, Jordan describes the tree climbing sequence as 'totally surreal – I mean you can't explain, you can't even say these elements are symbolic, they're just ... pleasing really'. Jordan's statement is a timely warning about the dangers of critical over-interpretation but a rejection of any symbolic potential for this sequence might be too hasty. In Carter's earlier radio play of the story, there is a clear emphasis on the symbolism of eggs:

Thirteen going on fourteen ... you are neither one thing nor the other, nor child nor woman, some magic, in-between thing, an egg that holds its own future in it. An egg not yet cracked against the cup. I am the very magic space that I contain. Like snow. Waiting. The clock inside me, that will strike once a month, not yet ... wound ... up ... I don't bleed. I can't bleed. (1996: 64–5)

It's difficult to imagine that, given Carter's involvement with the film, the symbols in the tree sequence did not have some conscious rationale behind them – and if they did not, their nature is ripe for a Freudian or Jungian analysis of archetypal symbols such as the tree, serpent and eggs. But even if there was no specific intent behind the sequence, the result is in keeping with Carter's celebration of the oral folk tradition. For Carter, it was important that the reader could transform the tale and that meaning was not fixed (she delighted in telling her own tales by giving public readings):

> I try, when I write fiction, to think on my feet – to present a number of propositions in a variety of different ways, and to leave the reader to construct her own fiction for herself from the elements of my fictions. (Reading is just as creative an activity as writing and most intellectual development depends upon new readings of old texts.) (Quoted in Crofts 2003: 46)

Leaving space for the reader/spectator is, of course, a risky strategy and has resulted in some (feminist) critics suggesting Carter does not go far enough in subverting the original tales – her playful irony does not demolish the dominant patriarchal structures. Nonetheless, *The Company of Wolves* remains a remarkable reworking of a classic story and in making this revision, in light of changes in attitudes towards women and sexuality, the film is able to maintain something of the oral tradition of folklore – telling and retelling tales to meet the needs of differing individuals within a community rather than locking any one interpretation in place, as is typical of the institutionalised fairy tale. The film's Chinese puzzle box structure (as Jordan's DVD commentary describes it) of tales within tales is not unique of course – indeed, such a structure is central to the source material of our next major genre of fantasy film: the *Arabian Nights* adaptation.

The Arabian Nights film

The tales collectively known as *The Arabian Nights* (or *The Thousand and One Nights*) have fascinated Western audiences since they gained widespread popularity in the early eighteenth century. In 1887, Robert Louis Stevenson, the great adventure story writer (who would work on his own collection of stories inspired by *The Arabian Nights*: *The New Arabian Nights* (1882) and *Island Nights' Entertainments* (1893)) wrote:

> There is one book ... more generally loved than Shakespeare, that captivates in childhood, and still delights in age – I mean the ARABIAN NIGHTS – where you shall look in vain for moral or for intellectual interest. No human face or voice greets us among that

wooden crowd of kings and genies, sorcerers and beggarmen. Adventure, on the most naked terms, furnishes forth the entertainment and is found enough. (2002: 160)

The fascination with all things Oriental, driven by the imperialist expansionism of the eighteenth and nineteenth centuries into Africa, South Asia and the Middle East, fuelled the popularity of *The Arabian Nights* in the West, and the newly-emergent technology of cinema, with its thirst for stories that would appeal to audiences, would soon draw on the tales. Méliès, predictably, was among the first to produce an *Arabian Nights* film with *Le Palais des mille et une nuits* (*The Palace of a Thousand and One Nights*, 1905) and others would follow, including *Aladdin and the Wonderful Lamp* (1917) and *Ali Baba and the Forty Thieves* (1918), before Douglas Fairbanks' lavish 1924 version of *The Thief of Bagdad*. Fairbanks' film echoed the potent combination of Arabia, romance and Rudolph Valentino in *The Sheik* (1921), which, although not featuring any of the magical elements of the *Arabian Nights*, maintained the association between an Arab setting and exotic adventure. Such was *Arabian Nights* fever at this time, in the US at least, that the mock-Arabian town of Opa-locka was built in Florida in the mid-1920s – a town where people dressed up as *Arabian Nights* characters and streets were given names like 'Ali Baba Avenue'. Opa-locka was officially incorporated in 1926 – the same year that Terry Ramsaye's history of film, *A Million and One Nights: A History of the Motion Picture*, was published, explicitly linking cinema and the *Arabian Nights* in its title.

It was not just Hollywood, however, that was inspired by the *Arabian Nights* as the basis for a film. Released in 1926, *Die Abenteuer des Prinzen Achmed* (*The Adventures of Prince Achmed*) is one of the great achievements of the pre-synchronous sound era and the first feature film by the German silhouette animator Lotte Reiniger, part of the Berlin art community. Work on the film commenced when Reiniger was still only 23 and took three years to complete with Reiniger designing, cutting and moving all the characters herself against backgrounds by Walter Ruttmann. Reiniger's characters were drawn from the stockpile of *Arabian Nights* figures – Aladdin and the Genie of the Lamp, an exotic princess, wicked sorcerer, the magic ebony horse and so on. The film has often been described as the first feature-length animated film but that status is not without qualification – earlier films, notably from Argentina, have also been proposed as the first but they no longer exist and their length is uncertain; Reiniger's film is the oldest *surviving* feature-length animation. *The Adventures of Prince Achmed* made genuine advancements, however, particularly in its use of multi-planar camerawork, which enabled several planes or fields of movement to take place simultaneously, giving an otherwise two-dimensional world a sense of depth (in sequences such as Prince Achmed's flight on the magic horse through the storm clouds and stars). The stop-motion approach used by Reiniger was developed further in relation to the *Arabian Nights* through the work of Ray Harryhausen, showcased in films often produced but not directed by the animator. Inspired by Willis O'Brien's work on *King Kong*, Harryhausen's combinations of model animation with live-action elements, which came fully to the fore in *The Beast from 20,000 Fathoms* (1954), were employed in his first colour feature, *The 7th Voyage of Sinbad* (1958), and he would return to the *Arabian Nights* on two more occasions with *The Golden Voyage of Sinbad* (1974) and *Sinbad and the Eye of the Tiger* (1977).

All of the *Arabian Nights* films mentioned so far, however, are not in keeping with much of the content of the actual tales in their earliest forms. Indeed, the writer and *Arabian Nights* scholar Robert Irwin has asserted that 'most filmed adaptations of stories from the *Nights* are frankly trashy' before acknowledging that 'a few, including the two versions of *The Thief of Bagdad* (1924 and 1940) and Pasolini's *Il fiore delle mille e una notte* [*Arabian Nights*, 1974], rank high among the masterpieces of world cinema' (2004: 292). The vast majority of *Arabian Nights* films focus on the linear adventures of a central heroic figure – Aladdin, Sinbad, Prince Achmed, the Thief – all of which give us the familiar story device of the male protagonist, the active hero figure, who propels the action and is typical of so many Hollywood narratives. The original tales, however, were far more varied than this standard approach and are framed by the linking device of Scheherazade, telling tale after tale in order to maintain the interest of a cuckolded Sultan who, having been betrayed by his first wife, vows that all his future wives will be executed after one night so that he cannot be betrayed again. Scheherazade will live for as long as her inventiveness in storytelling can last and the Sultan is compelled to keep her alive so that he can hear the next part of her story as she cunningly ends on a cliffhanger each night.

The tales Scheherazade and her characters tell are remarkably diverse – as Irwin notes, they cannot all be covered by the generic label of fairy tales (which is how they have tended to be presented in the West) and the collection includes:

> Long heroic epics, wisdom literature, fables, cosmological fantasy, pornography, scatological jokes, mystical devotional tales, chronicles of low life, rhetorical debates and masses of poetry. A few tales are hundreds of pages long; others amount to no more than a short paragraph. (Irwin 2004: 2)

Little of this diversity has been captured by *Arabian Nights* films. One of the great structural features of *The Arabian Nights* is that stories unfold within stories – as Scheherazade tells one story she introduces a new character who tells their story to a character within the world of the story until it becomes difficult to tell where one story has ended and another begun. Few screen adaptations have kept the Scheherezade/Sultan framing device (Hallmark Entertainment's mini-series *Arabian Nights* (2000) is a rare example), in part, because it results in a narrative structure at odds with the needs of an adventure story such as *The 7th Voyage of Sinbad* whose emphasis is on action and keeping the narrative flowing forwards rather than the stop/starts and digressions of the original source. The Scheherazade/Sultan plot, instigated by adultery and multiple executions, also underlines the tales' origins as stories told by adults to adults. As with the fairy tale, the *Arabian Nights* have tended to be transformed into children's stories in the West. In fact, much of what we take for granted in the tales is the product of a Western editorial decision. The tales come from a variety of sources: chiefly Persian, Indian and Chinese – with stories told and distributed by word of mouth, passed along trade routes or overheard in market places, spanning a journey from China to Egypt. By the tenth century a collection of the stories was already in existence but it was two later collections that secured the tales' popularity in Europe: Antoine Galland's 1704 edition and Sir Richard Burton's ten volume set published in 1885. The two collections are wildly different. Galland added the stories of Aladdin, Ali Baba and the voyages of Sinbad (from Persia) but, as Irwin suggests, there is some doubt over whether Aladdin and Ali Baba are authentic tales or European inventions (see 2004: 17–18). If Galland removed most of the sex and pornography from the tales then Burton's collection revelled in it and opportunities for scatological humour, as well as expressing Burton's racism and misogyny.

Compared with Burton's bawdy collection, the tone and content of most *Arabian Nights* films is that of family entertainment, from Alexander Korda's *Thief of Bagdad* to Disney's *Aladdin* (1992). But, although seemingly innocuous, these Western adventures in the exotic Middle East, with white actors playing Middle Eastern heroes such as Sinbad and white actors in face paint usually playing the evil sorcerer or untrustworthy Sultan, have all contributed to the discourse of Orientalism. The key figure here is the late Edward Said whose 1978 book outlined the ways in which Orientalism functioned to create an imaginative geography of the Middle and Far East that reassured Western nations of their own perceived superiority.

For Said, Orientalism was (and is) the means by which the major colonialist countries (namely, Britain, France and the US) represented, discussed and justified their imperialist activities in North Africa, Asia and the Middle East. A Palestinian educated in the West, Said's initial studies into Orientalism were concerned with travel writing about the East rather than film but others (such as Bernstein & Studlar (1997)) have applied his work to the moving image. At the root of Orientalism, Said argued, was the fact that it was less about the actuality of the East than it was about affirming the dominant values and ideologies of the West: 'The Orient has helped to define Europe (or the West) as its contrasting image, idea, personality, experience' (1995: 1–2).

The Orient became a catch-all term – a means of homogenising a vast and diverse landscape, barely distinguishing between differences in culture at a national (let alone regional) level. And it is a discourse that is played out again and again, asserting claims or perpetuating beliefs about the Oriental – whether the geographical landscape or the people inhabiting it. As Said details at length, the portrayal and discussion of the Orient in this literature contributed to a recurring set of themes and damaging characteristics – the Orient was portrayed as being despotic, populated by men who were often feminised and weak yet still threatening to white, Western women, with the landscape sharing similar traits to the Oriental female:

> Ideas about the Orient can be characterised as exclusively manifest differences ... the separateness of the Orient, its eccentricity,

The sensual and malleable Oriental female: Peri Banu in *The Adventures of Prince Achmed* (1926)

its backwardness, its silent indifference, its feminine penetrability, its supine malleability ... This is especially evident in the writing of travellers and novelists: women are usually the creatures of a male power-fantasy. They express unlimited sensuality, they are more or less stupid, and above all they are willing. (1995: 206–7)

For all its exquisite craftsmanship and charm, a film such as *The Adventures of Prince Achmed* is very much in keeping with the features identified by Said, particularly in relation to the characters of the childlike but lascivious Chinese Emperor and the Princess Peri Banu. Peri Banu exemplifies the sensual and passive Oriental woman. Having been ravished by each of the Princess's hand-maidens (who end up fighting over him), Prince Achmed spies on Peri Banu bathing in a pool and steals her magic cloak of feathers, leaving her naked, as he abducts her to a distant Chinese mountain-top where she accepts without argument his plea that she become his wife.

The more abstract representational nature of Reiniger's silhouette animation (skin colour and, to a certain extent, physiognomy do not have the signifying potential they would in other forms of animation or live action) makes the film less troubling than more recent examples of Oriental fantasies such as Disney's *Aladdin* or Steven Spielberg's *Indiana Jones and the*

Temple of Doom (1984). Erin Addison argues that the portrayal of Princess Jasmine in the Disney film, although pseudo-feminist, contributes to a 'deeply racist' work that embodies two American cultural strategies:

The first is a domestic strategy which shapes gender conceptions: the mystification of power through romantic love, and the packaging of romantic loves as freedom for women. The second is foreign policy: *Aladdin*'s political strategy protracts the complex American metaphor of a 'free marketplace, pure of political intent or impact', where wealth and opportunity are the birthrights of 'free' individuals. In that ideological marketplace, Muslim women are prizes to be won. (1993: 19)

More overt than *Aladdin*'s subtext is the portrayal of India in *Indiana Jones and the Temple of Doom* (which is not an *Arabian Nights* film). As Kaizaad Kotwal (2005) outlines, the film's portrayal of Kali worshippers as black magic occultists who eat live snakes, human eyeballs and monkey brains, apart from being historically inaccurate ('Kali worshippers like most Hindus are staunch vegetarians and never ate monkeys or snakes in any form because they are revered in their polytheistic traditions'), feeds into the film's endorsement of 'ideologies of colonialism and hegemonic notions of racial superiority' and a 'post-colonial misrepresentation of India, its cultures, religions and ancient traditions' under a veil of 'seemingly pure fantasy'.

One of the most problematic of all *Arabian Nights* films in terms of Orientalism is Pier Paolo Pasolini's *Il fiore delle mille e una notte*. Described by Robert Irwin as 'one of the most intelligent of modern interpreters of the *Nights*' (2004: 200), Pasolini manages to make a film that both adheres to the nature and structure of the original tales in a way not attempted previously by a screen adaptation and yet simultaneously engages with some of the most troubling practices and excesses of Orientalism. The film was the final part of Pasolini's *trilogia della vita* or 'Trilogy of Life', following on from *Il Decameron* (*The Decameron*, 1971) and *I racconti di Canterbury* (*The Canterbury Tales*, 1972). A Communist and homosexual, Pasolini rejected the conventions of mainstream cinema and opposed what he saw as bourgeois consumer culture and the colonisation of the body. These principles inform the aesthetic and conceptual strategies that he employed in the trilogy, which he claimed, at the time, represented the 'most ideological films I have ever made' (quoted in Rumble 1994: 210).

Right from the start of the film, Pasolini marks his *Arabian Nights* as different from other films in the genre. Most *Arabian Nights* films begin with a title sequence that promises a world of mystery and excitement, both visually and musically. For example, *The 7th Voyage of Sinbad* opens with colourful pseudo-Orientalist paintings depicting extraordinary creatures, rolling seas and stylised lettering. Similarly, Bernard Herrmann's score for the same film, although making use of the Javanese pelog scale common to gamelan music, contains a host of Oriental musical clichés that correspond to those Paul Robinson identifies as being typical of musical Orientalism in his study of Verdi's *Aida*. These include 'sinuous irregularity, long legato lines, close intervals, chromatic harmonies and subdued woodwind orchestration … distant harps … and a curling arabesque' (1993: 135–8). Pasolini's title sequence is the antithesis of this approach (and is in keeping, visually, with the title sequences of his other films): a plain background and simple font over which we hear distant street chatter and song. Pasolini's credits thus do not immediately exoticise the Oriental landscape with obvious signs – and nor do they tell us where we are or attempt to give us any clues about the stories that are about to unfold. Similarly, rather than portraying the Orient as an undifferentiated mass, Pasolini's diegesis is impressively diverse and takes place across several countries, with distinctly different cultures, architecture, soundscapes and ethnicities, as characters and stories travel from region to region. The effect may not be so obvious to the spectator used to literal devices such as onscreen text informing them that they are in 'Basra 800 AD' or wherever, but Pasolini's decision to shoot different stories in Ethiopia, Iran, Yemen and Nepal goes some way towards his film having something of the cultural diversity of the original collection of tales, which gathered stories from across the Middle and Far East.

The film's narrative structure is also notable in that it maintains the 'tales within tales' structure of the original *Arabian Nights*. The Scheherazade/Sultan framing device is not used but Pasolini employs an alternative linking thread in the form of Zumurrud (Ines Pellegrini) and Nur ed Din's (Franco Merli) plotline – perhaps not surprisingly, given his ideological sensibilities, Pasolini replaces the original framing device and its emphasis on the royal court with a relationship between a black slave girl and a naïve youth. This runs through the whole film and provides the jumping-off point for a series of tales – told first by Zumurrud and then various characters Nur ed Din encounters, including characters within a story telling a story. All of these devices are in keeping with Pasolini's rejection of mainstream cinematic codes and conventions. Consequently, the favoured characters of most Western/Hollywood *Arabian Nights* films, the heroic individuals such as Sinbad and Aladdin, are conspicuous by their absence. There are no active, heroic male characters in control of their own destiny – the men are often reliant on women for advice and instruction (and often ignore that instruction with disastrous consequences) – and the one male character who appears to be a heroic individual, Prince Tagi (Francesco Paolo Governale), uses deception in order to win the hand of the Princess Dunya (Abadit Ghidei).[1] The film's true hero is the slave girl, Zumurrud, who does determine her future (she mocks the men in the market bidding to purchase her and chooses her own master – Nur ed Din), escapes from the Forty Thieves, masquerades as the King of a distant realm and engineers her joyous reunion with Nur ed Din, having been abducted and separated as a result of his ineptitude and failure to follow her instructions.

The film would seem then to be a thoughtful interpretation of the original (adult) tales that manages to be remarkably authentic and avoids the Eurocentric pitfalls of most Western films based on the *Arabian Nights*.

The heroic slave girl: Zumurrud in Pasolini's *Arabian Nights* (1974)

Zumurrud is active, intelligent and resourceful – a far cry from the supine malleability Said asserts is typical of the women in Orientalist literature. But Pasolini's film is deeply problematic. If Zumurrud is a refreshing characterisation, other women in the film, disappointingly, tend to fall into the clichés detailed by Said – if they are not lustful women waylaying hapless men then they sacrifice their own existence (Aziza (Tessa Bouche)) or are psychotics such as Budur, who castrates Aziz (Ninetto Davoli) on the grounds that if she can no longer have him then no one can. The portrayal of sex and sexuality is at the root of the film's troubling Orientalism. In the Trilogy of Life, Pasolini sought to challenge bourgeois ideology by depicting and celebrating a simple, uncorrupted sexuality (and, in *Il fiore delle mille e una notte*, would draw on authentic source material in the form of seventeenth century erotic Rajput miniatures from the *Koka Shastra*), with the body being central to his 'search for some human essence or activity that has not been rationalised or commodified by the culture of consumer capitalism' (Rumble 1995: 20). As Patrick Rumble summarises:

> He celebrates ... [a] 'peasant' society, that of the Third World, with which he came to identify more and more in his own life. For Pasolini, it was a society still on the margins of consumer capitalism, where the bodies and imaginaries of the people had yet to be fully 'homologated' by the culture of neocapitalism ... non-Western societies and traditions exist as cultural hold-outs providing a potential point of resistance to the cultural hegemony of the economic centre. Thus, the Oriental miniatures that he brings to life in his film should be taken as emblematic of this form of cultural resistance. (1994: 217)

But this is an extremely dangerous strategy when dealing with representations of non-Western culture by a Western director, whatever their non-Western sympathies.

Although the film makes use of non-professional actors from the countries where it was filmed (Nepal, Iran, Yemen and Ethiopia) and thus offers them agency (rather than the usual Hollywood practice of white actors 'browning-up' to appear Arabian), this progressive step is compromised in two key ways. The first is through all the voices being dubbed in Italian (the default practice in Italian cinema but one Pasolini could have resisted); the second is the manner in which the local non-professional actors are often positioned before the camera, as Maurizio Viano (1993) argues, smiling in the same way that has been captured on camera by every Western tourist vacationing in the Third World. Although local non-professional actors were employed, Pasolini entrusted the majority of the principal roles to actors from Italy. The filmmaker may have had the noblest of intentions but, for Viano, he was guilty of gross naïvety and a patronising and romanticised view of Third World sexuality:

> To be a European filming in the Middle or Far East is by no means an innocent deed to be taken lightly, for, as Edward Said argues, 'one belongs to a power with definite interests in the Orient, and, more important, one belongs to a part of the earth with a definite history of involvement in the Orient since the time of Homer' ... Third World faces and places are enlisted in what seems yet another version of old colonialist projections. (1993: 270–1)

If Pasolini intended the trilogy to be a challenge to consumerism and the body as commodity, the films resulted in pornographic imitations by the very industry Pasolini was attempting to attack from within. Perhaps it was awareness of what he had spawned that resulted in Pasolini appearing to renounce the trilogy shortly after its completion before work began on his next (and final) film, *Salò o le 120 giornate di Sodoma* (1975). Adapted from the Marquis de Sade's *120 Days of Sodom* (1785), *Salò* is a bleak view of the depths to which humanity could sink with none of the joy, however misguided, of Pasolini's *Arabian Nights* on display. *Il fiore delle mille e una notte* remains a brave attempt at a more faithful interpretation of the *Arabian Nights* but ultimately cannot escape the dangers of the discourse that has compromised so many other films in the genre.

Despite its former glories, the future of the *Arabian Nights* film is unclear. In his discussion of the *Arabian Nights* films of Ray Harryhausen, Joshua David Bellin relates each film to its respective socio-political context in terms of contemporaneous US foreign policy and attitudes towards the Middle East. Thus the uncertainty of the 1950s, during which the US remained cautious in its involvement in major incidents in the region such as the 1956 Suez crisis and 'the conception of the Middle East as deadly nemesis had not yet become fully ingrained in the American cultural imagi-nation' (2005: 79), is echoed, Bellin suggests, in *The 7th Voyage of Sinbad*: its portrayal of the perils of foreign entanglements through a hero who gets his men killed by leading them into dangerous situations; an ambiguous villain, the magician Sokurah, who is both 'the source of the problem [and] its only solution' (2005: 90). Conversely, the 1974 film *The Golden Voyage of Sinbad* presents an obviously malevolent sorcerer in the form of Koura that, Bellin argues, was consistent with a drastic change in American perceptions of the Arab world: 'far from seeming a nebulous, distant peril, it had come to appear a direct and immediate threat to American safety and sovereignty, a land of random terror and, with its vast oil reserves, terrible power' (2005: 93). That perception has only heightened in the years following the attacks of 9/11, with the appearance of a direct and immediate threat from the Arab world now a devastating reality. The old Orientalist fantasies of the Middle East, as a magical realm full of exotic women willingly offering themselves to bold adventurers, have been exposed as irrelevant when the evening news regularly reports insurgency, terrorism and death. Yet the stereotype of the passive Oriental female has only been exchanged for another stereotype – the Islamic extremist concealing an explosive device beneath her *jilbab*. Rewatching Korda's *The Thief of Bagdad* in 2008 is a potentially disquieting experience, as Western actors talk and walk freely about the film's fantasy portrayals of Baghdad and Basra, so removed from the two cities' dominant portrayal on contemporary Western news services post-2003. Tellingly, DreamWorks' animated feature from 2003, *Sinbad: Legend of the Seven Seas* (with Sinbad voiced by Brad Pitt), drew on sources from Greek myth (the tale of Damon and Pythius) rather than the Arabian originals, relocating Sinbad from Basra to the 'safer' territory of ancient Greece and the kingdoms of Syracuse and Thrace. *Sinbad: Legend of the Seven Seas* contains enjoy-able sequences and fine animation but performed disastrously at the box office, prompting its producer, Jeffrey Katzenberg, to claim that 'the idea of a traditional story being told using traditional animation is likely a thing of the past' (quoted in Holson 2003). But Katzenberg could also have been speak-ing about the traditional *Arabian Nights* film. It would be a brave (Western) filmmaker to revisit the *Arabian Nights* in the post-2003 geopolitical climate but perhaps, as with Sergio Leone's reworking of the classical western in the 1960s, the genre awaits a much-needed revisionist approach that inter-rogates the myths and fantasies of its Eurocentric past. With its emphasis on cultural reconciliation and co-existence, as well as a celebration of Arabic art, architecture and intellectual traditions, Michel Ocelot's beautiful animated feature, *Azur & Asmar: The Princes' Quest* (2006) points the way to an alternate direction.

Sword and sorcery

For many, fantasy cinema *is* sword and sorcery. Mobina Hashmi, Bill Kirkpatrick and Billy Vermillion observe that 'fantasy is most often associated with the swords-and-sorcerers-style epics of alternate realities' (2003: 1) and, similarly, Howard Andrew Jones (n.d.) commences his definition of the literary genre by commenting that 'those who have only a passing familiarity with fantasy fiction are apt to use the terms "fantasy" and "sword and sorcery" as though they are interchangeable'. The label 'sword and sorcery' brings with it a clear-cut pair of semantic features for the genre, but to apply the phrase as a catch-all term to any film in which sword-fighting and magic users are prominent risks denying the cultural specificities of particular genres whose tropes, heritage and ethos would be lost through assimilation into the category. To give an extreme example, King Hu's *Xia nu* (*A Touch of Zen*, 1969–71) and Richard Fleischer's *Red Sonja* (1985) both feature extensive scenes of sword-fighting, both emphasise swordswomen and characters with supernatural powers but the latter film has none of the cultural and spiritual depth of Hu's epic, which, as Héctor Rodríguez (1998) details, draws on traditional Chinese forms such as Beijing opera and landscape painting (*shanshui hua*). *A Touch of Zen* belongs to the *wuxia pian* genre (meaning 'chivalrous combat' or 'martial arts hero' film) whereas *Red Sonja* is a genuine, albeit camp, example of sword and sorcery. The term then does not (and should not) apply indiscriminately to any film featuring wizards and warriors – sword and sorcery is a form of heroic fantasy with its own particular criteria.

What, then, is sword and sorcery? The term originated from its own practitioners rather than being invented by critics or the industry. The term's 'creation myth' is that it was first proposed in 1961 in a letter, published in the 6 April edition of the journal *Ancalagon*, from the celebrated American fantasy author Fritz Leiber, creator of the Fafhrd and Gray Mouser stories set in and around the city of Lankhmar. Leiber had written in response to a letter from the British writer Michael Moorcock (author of the epic Elric of

Melniboné saga (1961–)), who had requested a name for the genre to mark it out from other types of fantasy fiction. Leiber recommended sword and sorcery as a 'popular catchphrase'.

This referencing of the popular is crucial to sword and sorcery and its differentiation from epic or high fantasy (exemplified by Tolkien's *The Lord of the Rings*), which has a more sober tone. Sword and sorcery finds its roots in the Conan the Barbarian stories of Robert E. Howard written in the 1930s for the American pulp magazine *Weird Tales*. At its heart, it is a populist genre. The defining features of sword and sorcery, according to the impressive web resource on the genre at swordandsorcery.org, relate to its environment, protagonists, obstacles and story structure:

The Environment: Sword and sorcery fiction takes place in lands different from our own, where technology is relatively primitive, allowing the protagonists to overcome their martial obstacles face-to-face. Magic works, but seldom at the behest of the heroes. More often sorcery is just one more obstacle used against them and is usually wielded by villains or monsters. The landscape is exotic; either a different world, or far corners of our own.

The Protagonists: The heroes live by their cunning or brawn, frequently both. They are usually strangers or outcasts, rebels imposing their own justice on the wilds or the strange and decadent civilizations which they encounter. They are usually commoners or barbarians; should they hail from the higher ranks of society then they are discredited, disinherited, or come from the lower ranks of nobility (the lowest of the high).

Obstacles: Sword and sorcery's protagonists must best fantastic dangers, monstrous horrors, and dark sorcery to earn riches, astonishing treasure, the love of dazzling members of the opposite sex, or the right to live another day.

Structure: Sword and sorcery is usually crafted with traditional structure, meaning that it isn't stream-of-consciousness, slice-of-life, or any sort of experimental narrative – it has a beginning, middle, and end; a problem and solution; a climax and resolution.

> Most important of all, sword and sorcery moves at a headlong pace and overflows with action and thrilling adventure. (Anon.: n.d.)

Following these criteria, then, *The Lord of the Rings* does not qualify as sword and sorcery. The objectives for the Fellowship are more altruistic than a quest for treasure and romance: the Ring must be destroyed in order to gain the 'astonishing treasure' of freedom for the entire world of Middle-earth and this victory comes at a cost – Frodo is so scarred by his experiences that he cannot remain at peace in his homeland to enjoy the 'treasure' he has helped win; the structure of the book is less populist and in places quite ponderous (as Tom Shippey observes, there are 'occasions where Tolkien himself seems to forget, or ignore, some of the very basic axioms of narrative' (2005: 413)). The protagonists are also different from the figures characteristic of sword and sorcery. Joseph McCullough (n.d.) notes that Tolkien's protagonists are often 'reluctant adventurers', particularly Frodo, who is not driven by a wanderlust for the adventuring life. Yet if the book is quite distinct from sword and sorcery then the first film in the trilogy, *The Fellowship of the Ring*, contains moments that are more in keeping with the genre through a greater emphasis on combat than is in Tolkien's text (a number of battle scenes are far more elaborate and drawn-out than the corresponding scenes in the book) and a tone and pace that is also more dynamic and draws on populist genres. Once the Fellowship is formed and embarks on its quest to destroy the Ring, the film's streamlined narrative follows a more straightforward action/adventure path through a series of obstacles and perilous locales. This first film in the trilogy also has a central character, Aragorn, a ranger living and foraging in the wild, who operates as the warrior-outcast from society typical of literary sword and sorcery. Aragorn does not remain an outsider – by the end of the third film he has accepted his royal heritage and assumed his position as the head of society but in *The Fellowship of the Ring* this future is only hinted at and the film, as Kristin Thompson suggests, can seem to some 'a gallery of battles and monsters' (2003: 47).

Sword and sorcery came to prominence as a cinematic genre in the early 1980s following a decade that, for some critics of film fantasy, had not been particularly bountiful. Writing at the end of the 1970s, Frederick S. Clarke, the founder of *Cinefantastique*, concluded that:

The fantasy genre during the decade, particularly in the latter half, seemed always on the verge of the type of explosion that horror and science fiction films had undergone – but no such boom ever materialised, probably because no commercial super hit in the genre could be pointed at to catalyse filmmakers into action and investment. On the contrary, there were more than a few commercial and artistic disasters in the field during the '70s that may have served to postpone the entry of a trend in fantasy films that seems to be waiting in the wings. (1979: 73)

Clarke would be proven right – there were several fantasy films waiting to appear that had been in lengthy development phases throughout the 1970s, including *Excalibur* and *Conan the Barbarian*. Clarke identified the 1976 remake of *King Kong* as doing damage to the perception of fantasy films and, conversely, *Star Wars*, with its mythic and heroic impulse wrapped in science fiction trappings, as boosting the fortunes of fantasy projects. By the end of the decade, fantasy was perceived to be on the rise. Interviewed in 1979, Michael Powell discussed his desire to film Ursula Le Guin's *Earthsea* trilogy noting that it would 'fit perfectly into the current trend of big pictures full of myths, legends and fairy tales' (quoted in Kelley 1979: 80). An animated film of (part of) *The Lord of the Rings* appeared in 1978 followed by a series of fantasy films centred on heroic figures and/ or quest narratives in magical realms: *Hawk the Slayer, Excalibur, Clash of the Titans* (1981), *Dragonslayer, Conan the Barbarian, The Sword and the Sorcerer* (1982), *The Beastmaster, The Dark Crystal, Sword of the Barbarians* (1983), *Fire and Ice* (1983), *Krull* and *Deathstalker* (1983).

This wave of early 1980s fantasy was varied in quality, tone and genre. *Excalibur, Clash of the Titans, Dragonslayer, The Dark Crystal* and *Krull* belong to epic and heroic fantasy rather than sword and sorcery whereas films such as *The Beastmaster* or the Italian *Sword of the Barbarians* are derivative productions trading on the legacy of Robert Howard's Conan. *Conan the Barbarian* emerges as the one genuine example of sword and sorcery cinema in the 1980s fantasy boom that has a level of sincerity and thoughtful production design (by Ron Cobb) lacking in most films released in its wake. Starring Arnold Schwarzenegger in the title role, *Conan the Barbarian* was directed by John Milius with a script developed by Milius from an earlier draft by Oliver Stone. Milius's approach to the project was to invest Conan's world with a sense of history and reality, in keeping with Howard's own fusion of history and mythology, downplaying the fantasy elements and grounding the film in a primal earthiness – an approach that Peter Jackson would endorse for *The Lord of the Rings* some twenty years later. Conan is mistrustful of magic and civilisation (the city is introduced to him in the film as 'civilisation – ancient and wicked'), he exists instead, and is at home, in the wilderness. In this sense, Conan is akin to figures such as Ethan Edwards in John Ford's 1956 western *The Searchers* or John Rambo in *First Blood* (1982) – loners who roam either outside of or on the periphery of society. The cult of individualism expressed by these films is at the heart of the sword and sorcery protagonist. For McCullough, these figures are 'free from all constraint':

> Their stature and skill mean they are free from the tyranny of other men. Their birth and raising free them from the morals and mores of society, and the lack of higher powers unbinds them from any concept of fate. Thus the heroes of sword and sorcery become the true representatives of free-will, and through their stories, readers are able to imagine the capabilities and the triumphs of men who are completely free to chart their own destiny. This is likely why sword and sorcery throughout the years has often appealed to a teenage crowd, who feel they are suffering from the pointless tyranny of the elders; while the rest of heroic fantasy, with its duties and obligations, has historically appealed to an older audience who are aware of the realities of such notions. (n.d.)

Such characteristics open the sword and sorcery genre up to accusations of reactionary conservatism and (at worst) harbouring fascist tendencies. The genre's cinematic emergence in the early 1980s coincided with a shift in America towards the political conservatism of the Reagan era. Conan's principle of might is right and his conviction to trust in nothing and no one other than the steel of his sword chimed with the prevailing mood in America. Michael Ryan and Douglas Kellner (1988: 217) relate the revival of a 'pre-Vietnam sense of patriotic jingoism and militarism' (generated in part by the 1979 Iran hostage crisis) to the rise of the New Right and what they describe as the 'return of the hero' in both politics (i.e. Ronald Reagan, a former actor from the 'golden age' of Hollywood) and popular culture, as a patriarch, entrepreneur and warrior. The heightened militarism of Reagan's foreign policy (most famously expressed in his 'Evil Empire' speech of 8 March 1983, likening the Soviet Union to the Evil Empire, and the 'Star Wars' speech of 23 March 1983, which outlined a new strategic defence initiative) made Conan's maxim that what is best in life is to 'crush your enemies, see them driven before you and hear the lamentation of their women' a recognisable clarion call. Unlike many myths and legends that lend themselves to fascist readings as a result of their emphasis on the elitist purity of the hero and some prophesied notion that he is 'the one', Conan is not pre-destined for greatness but is shaped and hardened through adversity (the onscreen use, before the action begins, of Friedrich Nietzsche's aphorism 'that which does not kill us makes us stronger' establishes the film's philosophy from the outset). Yet as Ryan and Kellner note, *Conan the Barbarian* remains a 'conservative fantasy projection' (1988: 225), consistent with Milius's wider body of work (such as his screenplay for the anti-liberal Harry Callahan in *Magnum Force* (1973), the sequel to *Dirty Harry* (1971), or his anti-Communist scare film *Red Dawn* (1984) which features a band of US youths fighting back against a Soviet invasion). Milius's film also 'articulates the rootless, nostalgic conservatism of the petit bourgeois, the lower middle class sector whose lack of a stable class or economic fix motivates an anxious yearning for stable order, simpler times, and a powerful authority to dispel the multiple fantasy threats that are the paranoid projections of economic and social security' (1988: 226). For better or worse, *Conan the Barbarian* paved the way for a host of fantasy films to come – as Michael Moorcock suggests on the DVD documentary *Conan: The Rise of a Fantasy Legend* (2005), the film 'set an entire genre into process' and 'virtually every plot that came after ... was some form of the Conan plot'. In one sense, Moorcock is right – *Conan the Barbarian* did give rise to a spate of sword and sorcery, barbarian and heroic fantasy films – but few shared the conceptual integrity and seriousness of intent of Milius's film (whatever one's interpretation of its politics). Milius was absent from the follow-up to *Conan the Barbarian*, *Conan the Destroyer*, and the tone of Richard Fleischer's sequel is knowing and tongue-in-cheek with less care given to creating a believable and coherent alternate world. Yvonne Tasker has commented on the tendency in these later fantasy films for minor characters to 'constantly comment on the action, acting to undercut the overblown figures of the heroes and

'Crush your enemies': conservative militarism in *Conan the Barbarian* (1982)

heroines' (1993: 28–9), and this trend is taken further in *Red Sonja*. As the decade progressed there were notable fantasy projects to demonstrate a vivid creativity or fresh approaches to familiar material – *Labyrinth* (1986) and *The Princess Bride* (1987) being two of the highlights – but by the end of the 1980s, the wave of sword and sorcery and heroic fantasy films had passed, concluding with films such as Lucasfilm's *Willow*, described by *Variety* as a 'bastardised' and 'derivative … medieval mishmash' (Anon. 1988). It would be more than ten years before a heroic fantasy film would be both a major critical and commercial success. As Peter Jackson put it following the first release in his Tolkien trilogy:

> I have always wanted to make a fantasy film. That genre is not really popular, and the studios don't really like it anymore. The best thing about this for me is that it has put me in the position of showing Hollywood studios that fantasy can be successful at the box office if it is done in a certain way. That for me is the proudest thing of these films – that I have taken a genre that I love, which Hollywood doesn't, and proved to them that it can be successful. (Quoted in Thompson 2003: 46)

In the next chapter, we will consider some of the 'certain ways' employed by filmmakers to create a successful portrayal and sense of fantasy, with varying degrees of box-office success.

3   REALISING FANTASY: AUDIO-VISUAL STYLE

'This is DYNAMATION!'

Throughout the pressbook for *The 7th Voyage of Sinbad* (1958), one word was emphasised as the principal reason for seeing this 'astounding' new film: DYNAMATION (the pressbook insisted on the capitalisation). The film was the first to feature Ray Harryhausen's stop-motion creations in Technicolor and showcased an array of monsters (including the Cyclops and Roc as well as a dragon and snake-woman). But the pressbook singled out one particular stop-motion sequence for special attention: Sinbad's duel with the skeleton. According to the pressbook, 'Only DYNAMATION could make this wonder of wonders come into reality on the screen. It's a swashbuckling fight between a swashbuckling human being and an equally swashbuckling skeleton' (Anon. 1958). Dynamation was the word given to describe Harryhausen's outstanding combination of live-action performers and stop-motion models interacting in the same frame. For the film's producer, Charles H. Schneer, Dynamation expressed the very essence of the medium:

> This process goes straight to the heart of the motion picture itself.
> It utilises the medium as a principal factor, not merely as a means
> of conveying a story. It liberates the imagination, opens new areas
> of entertainment ingenuity. It is basic motion picture. (In Ibid.)

In arguing that fantasy and visual effects were fundamental to cinema, Schneer was echoing the comments of William Cameron Menzies about his stylised art design for *The Thief of Bagdad* (1924):

> Oh, this is the realm of the pictures isn't it? This is the thing they can do – if they'd only see it! Realism is so unnecessary when we have at our disposal all the resources of the camera to produce effects that can only be rivalled by dreams. (Quoted in Anon. 1984: 18)

Schneer and Menzies are part of a long tradition in film that has expressed the fantasy impulse. As Neil Forsyth traces it, in his discussion of differing attempts to realise the supernatural in film adaptations of Shakespeare, this lineage stretches from the origins of cinema to the present day, taking in a wide variety of exponents along the way:

> What began with Méliès continued in the *grand guignol* ideas of Sergei Eisenstein and his 'montage of attractions', in Cocteau's surrealism, in experiments like James Stewart's dream of falling in Hitchcock's *Vertigo* and the final sequences of Kubrick's *2001*; it is manifest in animation, in the Spielberg-style special effects which have so outdistanced what Méliès could manage, and it survives especially in the immensely popular horror-movie genre, where ghosts and witches and diabolical possession are six-a-penny. (2000: 274–5)

Indeed, film, by its very nature, is founded on a trick – that of watching flowing continuous movement when in fact we are watching a series of still images flickering past us at 24 frames a second. As Forsyth suggests, it is often through attempts to portray the fantastic or distortions in reality that new film technology and techniques have been developed or employed – whether that is the 'dolly zoom' invented by Irmin Roberts for Hitchcock to represent James Stewart's acrophobia in *Vertigo* (1958), Kubrick's use of Garrett Brown's still-fledgling Steadicam to create an unsettling, floating supernatural gaze through the corridors of the Overlook hotel in *The Shining* (1980), or George Lucas's establishment of the visual effects company Industrial Light and Magic in 1975, which has produced groundbreaking developments in visual effects, particularly in relation to computer-generated imagery (CGI). Often pioneered in fantasy-related films, these advances have gone on to be used outside the fantasy field. This chapter will focus on some of the audio-visual methods used in fantasy film and identify some of the most distinctive exponents of the cine-fantastic. Rather than being simply a list of special effects and 'making of' details, the interest here is in how audio-visual style can contribute to an effective sense of fantasy and the fantastic, prompting us to question the nature of what we see and hear in a film.

Fantasy landscapes and space

One of the greatest challenges facing fantasy filmmakers is the construction and portrayal of the worlds and spaces in which their narratives take place. This challenge is more acute for those films in fantasy genres, particularly heroic fantasy, sword and sorcery and fairy tale films, which feature alternative worlds with different landscapes and architectures to our own. Constructing that alternate world is challenging enough but populating it as well, with enough inhabitants to create a sense that it is also a functioning world and not just limited to isolated set-pieces, is an undertaking that has traditionally been financially prohibitive.

There have been various approaches to constructing fantasy worlds. The rarest, due to time and cost, is to start completely from scratch and build a world in which everything is different to our own. Jim Henson's *The Dark Crystal* (1982) is a remarkable piece of alternate world-building in this respect and a project largely motivated by the challenge to create a world in which, as the pressbook explained, 'there would be no "reality" as we know it, either human or natural, and yet everything would be totally, palpably "real"' (Anon. 1982). With no human characters, all aspects of *The Dark Crystal*'s predominantly studio-bound world are original pieces of design. 'The result', promised the pressbook, 'is an astonishing visual experience … that will be seen as a remarkable advance in the use of the film medium … Here everything is alive. Plant and tree have the gift of speech, water murmurs the music of forgotten days, and the possible replaces the impossible as mountain and rock become moving beings' (ibid.). If *The Dark Crystal* is totally alien, Neil Jordan's *The Company of Wolves* creates an effective blurring between what is real and unreal through its combination of studio set and live inhabitants for those scenes set in the forest, which dominates both the film and Rosaleen's dreams. The film creates a world that only *seems* real by fusing the authentic (live wolves, owls and frogs) with the fake (giant toadstools, stylised tree trunks and plumes of studio mist), which functions as an effective correlate to the film's central theme of people not necessarily being what they appear to be. If Jordan takes an artificial world and adds real elements to it, the portrayal of landscape in several of the films of Michael Powell and Emeric Pressburger employs the reverse process – taking existing natural settings and then augmenting them through evocative cinematography (and music) to create a heightened reality. In films such as *A Canterbury Tale* (1944), *I Know Where I'm Going!* (1945) and *Gone to Earth* (1950), as Stella Hockenhull (2005) has discussed, the landscape takes on a mystical, romantic quality. *Gone to Earth* is particularly notable for several moments of animism, with stone and wood invested with a sense of being alive and embodying ancient spirits – an effect created without recourse to any advanced puppetry, CGI or animatronics and achieved instead through careful selection of trees with distinctive features and low-key high-contrast lighting. Similarly, in *Excalibur*, John Boorman creates the 'spirits of wood and stream' by enhancing the already beautiful landscape of County Wicklow in Ireland with an ethereal green glow, provided by off-camera lighting. Boorman's use of in-camera methods to give the landscape a magical aura was replaced by post-production techniques on Peter Jackson's *The Lord of the Rings*, where editing software is used throughout the three films to digitally grade the colours and brightness of the actual footage, giving, for example, the Shire vivid greens in order to emphasise its status as a rural paradise.

When *The Thief of Bagdad* was released in 1924, the *Daily Express* enthused that 'there never have been such sweeping panoramas and perspectives, such immense spaciousness … ceaseless and vast' (Anon. 1924a) but the same admiring comments can be made about Jackson's *The Lord of the Rings*. The Jackson films pay close attention to Tolkien's richly detailed accounts of the geography and landscape of Middle-earth to portray an alternate expansive space quite unlike and far superior to anything realised in film before. Improvements in CGI, a tool that was simply not available to filmmakers until its initial use by Industrial Light and Magic in the 1980s, have made it possible for fantasy worlds to be viewed from every available perspective contributing to a sense that they

Advances in model shots and fantasy landscapes: the approach to Camelot in *Excalibur* (1981) and Minas Tirith in *The Return of the King* (2003)

fully occupy their space and are not just viewable from a specific vantage point. Traditional methods of putting large-scale constructions into existing landscapes would include the use of glass shots (whereby an enhancement to the landscape, a medieval castle for example, is painted onto a glass panel placed before the camera – the camera thus sees the painted element and the land around it) or forced perspective model shots – but these techniques require the camera to be fixed in place. CGI now allows a camera to roam around a digitally-enhanced landscape, viewing fantastic structures and geographical features (such as the two giant statues of the Argonath standing over the river Anduin in *The Fellowship of the Ring*) from all angles. Similarly, CGI enabled the vast landscapes in *The Lord of the Rings* to be convincingly populated as well. The trilogy pioneered the use of Massive (Multiple Agent Simulation System in Virtual Environment), a 3-D animation system developed by Stephen Regelous specifically for Weta Digital to provide the trilogy with large-scale battles involving hundreds of thousands of digitally-animated characters, each of which moves and interacts in relation to the characters around them.

Earlier attempts to portray epic fictional worlds on screen, such as *Excalibur* and *Conan the Barbarian*, although possessing great visual imagination, are limited in terms of the spaces they create and their ability to show the 'connective tissue' of landscape between key locations, as well as the populations inhabiting them. There is a marked difference between the portrayal of Camelot in *Excalibur* and, say, the walled city of Minas Tirith in *The Return of the King*. *Excalibur* is never quite able to establish Camelot as a convincing structure at the heart of a thriving kingdom – due principally to budgetary and technological limitations. Camelot tends to be seen in a fixed long-shot: a small model projected onto the camera lens via a mirror so that it appears to be nestling in the distant woods. Although an effective trick shot, Boorman is restricted as to what he can do with it – the camera has to remain locked in order to keep the image of the castle fixed in place. Boorman cannot track closer in to Camelot and establish the full majesty of Arthur's castle (for example, in a tracking shot following Lancelot (Nicholas Clay) as he approaches the kingdom on horseback with Perceval (Paul Geoffrey) hard on his heels and the castle growing in stature) without destroying the illusion (the moment the camera moves it leaves the reflected image of the castle behind). Camelot must remain a distant and barely discernible shape – 'only a model' as Patsy observes in *Monty Python and the Holy Grail* (1975). Advances in CGI and a superior budget, however, mean that Gandalf and Pippin's approach to the city of Minas Tirith is a vastly more convincing spectacle. A combination of actual set, miniatures and digital imagery, Minas Tirith is a stunning achievement but what fully convinces is its coherent occupation of space: the city is seen from a variety of angles and distances, always maintaining a consistent relationship to the surrounding geography.

The Lord of the Rings films are packed with reference points which aid the spatial orientation of the spectator. Throughout *The Return of the King* there is an outstanding attention to geographical detail and spatial consistency, which is essential if key elements of the narrative's multi-

Spatial reference points in *The Return of the King* (2003)

ple strands are to realise their dramatic potential. Space is crucial to *The Lord of the Rings* – we need to have a clear sense of the expansive landscapes at work and the distances between the significant landmarks in order to fully appreciate the heroic tasks being undertaken. Can an ailing Frodo (Elijah Wood) and Sam (Sean Astin) make it across the wastes of Mordor and up the volcanic slopes of Mount Doom to destroy the Ring? Can the Rohirrim come to the aid of Minas Tirith in time? If space is not established convincingly then these plot points risk losing much of their available impact. A good example of spatial reference points being established takes place in the scene where Frodo, Sam and Gollum approach the haunted city of Minas Morgul and a supernatural beacon erupts out of the Morgul tower into the sky. The beacon is seen in close proximity by the three travellers but is also witnessed by Gandalf and Pippin watching from the walls of Minas Tirith several miles away. As well as providing a moment of spectacle it also helps to establish space and distance, maintaining the malevolent presence of Mordor in the spectator's consciousness and thus the vulnerability of Minas Tirith as well – we now know just how close and exposed the city is to the forces of Mordor, which could be unleashed at any moment – so there is a dramatic function here too.

Not all fantasy films choose to establish a coherent sense of space in which we know the landscape as thoroughly as possible – for some, incoherent or ambiguous space is central to the fantasy effect being sought. Jackson's (sometimes excessive) elaborate helicopter shots ensure that much of the landscape of New Zealand as Middle-earth is objectified and known to us, offering majesty but few mysteries (see Butler (2007) for further discussion of the potential consequences of Jackson's camera style on the spectators' experience of the landscape in *The Lord of the Rings*) but a very different approach to space and landscape is evident in King Hu's epic *A Touch of Zen*. As Héctor Rodríguez has detailed, Hu draws on traditions in Chinese painting as well as Buddhist notions of 'perspectivism' to create an 'anti-rational' (rather than irrational) aesthetic in which our human experience of the world cannot be total. Unlike Jackson's camera, which floats above Middle-earth taking it all within its gaze (not unlike the all-seeing lidless eye of Sauron), Hu's visual style references a Chinese tradition of insisting on 'the primacy of spirit over denotation' to create an 'indeterminate, mysterious atmosphere' and occasionally 'clouded and magical space' via 'mist, backlighting, shallow focus, overexposed shots, chiaroscuro and the glittering reflections of sunlight on water' so that characters often wander within a 'deep, obscure, illimitable and oneiric space' (Rodríguez 1998: 85–6). In keeping with Chan Buddhism, Hu's portrayal of space and landscape as mysterious, and therefore still containing the potential to surprise, aligns it with the Chan goal 'to foster a complete realignment of experience: the bewildering dawning of a new and unexpected point of view popularly known as *wu* or enlightenment' (Rodríguez 1998: 89). If Jackson's approach in *The Lord of the Rings* encourages us to know and understand Middle-earth as a pseudo-historical reality and marvel at the logistical achievement in constructing it, Hu's more mysterious landscape 'confronts the viewer with the limits of human mastery' (Rodríguez 1998: 92) by not fixating on known objects and entities – nature is respected but key to that respect is that it cannot be fully known and controlled.

A less obvious creation of fantasy space is displayed in *Orphée* (1950), Jean Cocteau's updating of the myth of Orpheus in the Underworld seeking his lost lover, Eurydice. Orpheus is now a frustrated poet, Orphée, and resident on Paris's postwar Left Bank. In one sequence, Orphée (Jean Marais) follows Death (María Casares), in the form of a mysterious aristocratic Lady, through the streets of Paris but the journey and route he takes is a disruption of actual space – Cocteau employs subtle spatio-temporal elisions that are only noticeable if the spectator is familiar with the geography of Paris. The obvious fantasy element is the materialisation of the Lady out of thin air but this is an understandable example of Todorov's category of the marvellous (she is after all a supernatural entity). Following Todorov, the genuine *fantastic* moment is how Orphée gets from locations in Paris that are a mile apart in a couple of strides. As Roland-François Lack clarifies, in the DVD commentary, 'the discontinuity of place is overridden by the matching of the actors' movements' so it appears that Orphée's journey is continuous. Orphée would have to have travelled for at least ten minutes in reality but he is still on the same cigarette, suggesting, alongside the matching of movement, that virtually no time has elapsed at all. The effect is the construction of an impossible city out of real and well-known Parisian landmarks – the familiar becomes unfamiliar and no explanation is given. For Rosemary Jackson, in fantastic texts, 'classical unities of space, time and character are threatened with dissolution' (2003: 46) and filmmakers have explored the same themes with cinema being particularly adept at portraying spatio-temporal distortions. Orson Welles employs more jarring and explicit jumps in space than Cocteau for his adaptation of Franz Kafka's *The Trial* (1962), where doors open onto totally different environments and architecture, creating an illogical world in which mundane procedures such as stepping through a doorway become disorienting experiences. These transformations and distortions of reality are achieved through one of cinema's simplest and original effects: editing and montage.

Fantasy stylistics: montage, cinematography and mise-en-scène

J. R. R. Tolkien did not live to see the emergence of CGI but he expressed a dim view of 'mechanical' attempts to realise fantasy on stage (2001: 50). Dwell too long on a visual effect, often at the expense of narrative progression, and it risks losing its ability to disrupt our understanding of reality and for the audience to consider instead its realisation and execution as an effect. In his 1953 essay 'The Virtues and Limitations of Montage', André Bazin argued (in relation to the anthropomorphic animal films of Jean Tourane) that without the use of montage, the effect, however impressive:

> Would pass from being something imaginary to something real. Instead of delighting in a fiction, we would be full of admiration for a well-executed vaudeville turn. It is montage, that abstract creator of meaning, which preserves the state of unreality demanded by the spectacle. (2004: 45)

Montage (or editing), as Bazin noted, does not guarantee a successful illusion and creation of convincing fantasy – it still requires great precision, choreography and vision in matching shots so that the cuts and changes in elements do not seem too forced. Used poorly, montage can be just as obvious as an unconvincing piece of CGI or a clear outline and change in visual quality around an actor indicating that they are part of a process shot and not actually present in the landscape behind them. Used sensitively, CGI can be an extremely effective tool and its ability to reproduce difficult natural textures (fur, fire, flesh, for example) continues to improve. The realisation of the emaciated creature Gollum in *The Lord of the Rings* trilogy is an impressive fusion of the real and unreal, using motion capture devices to map actor Andy Serkis's facial and body movements onto a computer-animated model of Gollum, blurring the distinction between the human and non-human. In the main, however, spectacle has tended to be the enemy of Todorov's fantastic with its emphasis on hesitancy. In this section I want to outline some alternative approaches in visual style to the creation of a strong sense of fantasy.

In a meticulous analysis of Carl Theodor Dreyer's *Vampyr* (1932), Mark Nash proposed a film genre analogous to Todorov's literary fantastic: the cine-fantastic (see 1976: 30). For Nash, Todorov's hesitancy is achieved most effectively in film through the manipulation of the spectators' understanding of whose point of view (if any) the camera is providing at any given moment. In *Vampyr* the hesitancy centres on the protagonist, David (or, depending on the print, Allan) Gray (Julian West), and whether he is really experiencing the film's events as they unfold, or is dreaming them, or is already dead and we are being presented with an account of what has taken place. *Vampyr* alternates and creates a dialectic 'between the impersonal shots (those independent of Gray's perception) and the point-of-view structures in the film [which] is the major structure supporting the fantastic' (Nash 1976: 34). Does the camera's gaze belong to David Gray (as it clearly seems to at times)? Or does it belong to another presence within or outside the film's diegesis? The spectator is placed on shifting sands between objectivity and subjectivity, reality and unreality. Throughout the film, the nature and owner of the camera's gaze is called into question. Slavoj Žižek has discussed the function of this technique at length in relation to the films of Alfred Hitchcock, particularly Arbogast's murder in *Psycho* (1960), and in *The Birds* (1963). Žižek claims that Hitchcock is at his most unnerving when the spectator becomes aware that 'there is no possible subject within the space of diegetic reality who can occupy the point of view of this shot' (2001: 36). The result is an impossible subjectivity, which lends the preceding objectivity a 'flavour of unspeakable, monstrous evil' (ibid.) – what we thought was a reliable, detached view (belonging to what Žižek calls the 'absent one', someone, such as the director, in control of the gaze outside the diegesis) transforms into something malevolent (or vice versa).

The overall effect in *Vampyr* is a film that David Rudkin has described as 'visually the most transgressive in existence' (2005: 24). That transgressive quality is realised through the film's rejection, intentionally or otherwise, of what are now the long-established 'rules' and conventions of classical visual style. These conventions can become so entrenched in our film experience that when they are discounted the effect can be startling and even troubling. Such conventions include the principle of continuity editing, whereby shot follows shot in a logical and linear sequence that is designed to orientate the spectator and aid their understanding of the narrative, eye-line matching, point-of-view shots and the shot/reverse-shot or 180-degree rule. Shot/reverse-shot is one of the basic editing patterns in film, typically used in dialogue scenes to establish who is talking to whom (one shot, showing the talker, is followed by a reverse-shot showing who is being talked at). Breaking these conventions, for example, withholding the expected reverse-shot from a point-of-view shot so that we do not get to learn the identity of the gazer (a standard device in supernatural cinema as well as slasher and murder mystery films) is an effective means of generating suspense and an unsettling atmosphere or distorting the spectators' perception of the onscreen events. Conversely, rapid cutting between shots is used by King Hu in *A Touch of Zen* to create impossible actions and movements across space. David Bordwell refers to Hu's use of the 'glimpse' – that is, an image that we have barely enough time to be aware of. In some cases, Hu uses images that run for less than eight frames so that the spectator cannot take in their full content: 'we are allowed only a trace of the warriors' amazing feats. We do not see action as much as glimpse it' (Bordwell quoted in Rist 2007: 171).

A good example of non-continuity editing being used to create a sense of unreality is Jonathan Miller's film of *Alice in Wonderland* made for the BBC in 1966. The film is one of the finest evocations of dream logic, which Miller successfully creates through spatio-temporal jumps, slow-motion, repetition, reflections not corresponding to their source and incongruous elements of *mise-en-scène*. Alice's (Anne-Marie Mallik) initial encounter with the White Rabbit (Wilfred Brambell) creates an appearance of continuity and linearity but actually distorts space, time and logic. The White Rabbit appears in shot in the mid-ground of the frame and Alice sits up from her dozing, oblivious to his presence – but in the very next shot she is seen purposefully following the White Rabbit. We lack the 'making sense' or 'recognition' shot of seeing Alice notice the Rabbit and begin to follow him but it is an effective portrayal of dream logic where we often find ourselves in entirely different locations simultaneously or change our course of action without any apparent reason. Miller avoids obvious fantasy opportunities (the inhabitants of Wonderland are not actors in animal costumes) and opts for subtler disruptions of reality. As Alice follows the White Rabbit into Wonderland, in what is basically a chase sequence (even though both only walk briskly), there are jumps in location that do not quite make sense yet the overriding form of the linear pursuit gives us a familiar pattern with which we can make sense of the non-continuity editing and bizarre shifts in location.

All of the above examples use editing – and in some cases rapid montage – to create their transformations of reality. Yet montage is not essential to the aesthetics of fantasy. Although the spiritual intensity of his work has meant that he has not often been thought of as an exponent of the cine-fantastic, Andrei Tarkovsky excelled in portrayals of our world that transform it into a place full of luminous beauty, mystery, decay and terror. As Tarkovsky's own son, Andrei, commented about his father's aims as an artist, 'He tried to adjust your vision, it was all about vision,

Memory and temporal dissolution: the lateral tracking shot in *Nostalgia* (1983)

all his films are about the way you see things ... I think my father was this kind of man, a person who could rearrange reality and show you some totally different point of view' (quoted in Norton 2008: 41). Tarkovsky was opposed to montage and turned instead to (often extremely) long takes in order to create many of his most fantastic sequences. In doing so, as Benjamin Halligan argues, Tarkovsky employs a method (the long take) advocated by Bazin for its potential for realism, and uses it instead in such a way that 'problematises reality and privileges fantasy' (2006: 55). One of Tarkovsky's favoured shots is the slow, often imperceptible, tracking movement, forwards or backwards, a device that pulls us into the world of his films. Another of his signature moves is the lateral tracking shot, something he used throughout his cinema to blur the distinctions between dreams, memories and lived experience so that we can no longer be sure what is real and unreal. Natasha Synessios notes how Tarkovsky uses these lateral movements to 'suggest that past, present and future exist simultaneously, that time and space are not subject to the laws of logic' (2001: 50). Over the course of an extended lateral movement, figures within the frame are often left out of shot and then reappear later in the same movement in an entirely different place and yet they appear not to have moved. This device of having a character seeming to appear in more than one simultaneous space and time within a single shot is present in *Solyaris* (*Solaris*, 1972) as well as *Zerkalo* (*Mirror*, 1975), *Nostalghia* (*Nostalgia*, 1983) and *Offret* (*The Sacrifice*, 1986), Tarkovsky's final film.

Tarkovsky was not alone in recognising the fantastic potential of the long unedited take. Kenji Mizoguchi uses it to outstanding effect in *Ugetsu Monogatari* (1953) for Genjurô's (Masayuki Mori) return home. Genjurô enters the house, which seems uninhabited, and walks across an empty room in search of Miyagi, his wife. The camera pans after Genjurô as he leaves the room, explores the house then returns – as the camera comes back to rest it reveals that what had moments ago been an empty room is now occupied by Miyagi (Kinuyo Tanaka) cooking by a previously unlit fire. All of this is done in an unbroken camera movement – there is no edit to provide an easy explanation as to how this materialisation has taken place. As Robin Wood observes, 'the *frisson* this moment excites is due largely to the simple technical fact that there has been no cut, no dissolve, no editing of any kind: the impossible has happened before our eyes' (2006: 285). Wood's admiration for Mizoguchi is extensive: 'no filmmaker in my experience – not even Tourneur or Dreyer – has treated the supernatural with such delicacy and respect, with such subtle force of suggestion and so rigorous a refusal to sensationalise or vulgarise' (2006: 284). Contemporary Japanese horror and supernatural cinema are no strangers to sensation and vulgarity but there are exceptional examples in Japanese cinema of less explicit, albeit no less potent, approaches to fantasy and the supernatural. The vivid, stylised colours and hand-painted produc-

Nature's point of view: atypical *mise-en-scène* in *The Night of the Hunter* (1955)

tion design of Masaki Kobayashi's *Kwaidan* (1965) contrast strikingly with the black-and-white sensuality of Kaneto Shindô's *Onibaba* (1964) and *Kuroneko* (1968). *Kuroneko* combines overtly supernatural moments such as its feline she-demons flying through the air (courtesy of wire-work) with evocative natural imagery, mist, snow and burning suns, and simpler techniques that enhance reality ever so slightly (the she-demons' slow-motion leap over a pool in the forest) to create an erotic and tragic film that, like *Ugetsu Monogatari*, does not veer into gratuitous imagery.

Hesitancy can also be achieved through unusual compositions and improbable but not *impossible* arrangements of the *mise-en-scène*. Long before its more obvious manifestations of the supernatural begin to appear, *The Innocents* establishes a disturbing sickness of tone when Miss Giddens chances upon a stone cherub in the grounds at Bly. Her initial delight soon turns to disgust when a large insect emerges from the cherub's mouth, tainting the statue's innocence (and anticipating the film ahead as Miss Giddens becomes convinced that the two young children in her care are inhabited by perverted and malevolent non-corporeal forces, a possibility that is further alluded to through the cherub holding a pair of adult hands that are not attached to an actual body). Shot composition can also be effective. Both *The Company of Wolves* and *The Night of the Hunter* (1955), Charles Laughton's one-and-only idiosyncratic outing as director, create a sense of the fantastic through the unusual emphasis on aspects of the diegetic world that we would not normally expect to have primacy. In both films there are sequences where humans are talking/singing but do not have authority over the shot as we might expect (in the former, Rosaleen and her Granny's walk through the forest, and the children's night-time journey down the river in the latter) – the camera watches them in the distance from behind, respectively, tree branches and a spider's web with the emphasis on the creatures in the wood and the riverbank. This foregrounding of nature contributes to the sense of a world in which humans are not dominant (Derek Jarman takes a similar approach in the build-up to Ariel's first appearance in his film of *The Tempest* (1979)). None of the individual elements of the *mise-en-scène* in the examples above are so impossible as to be easily discounted as marvellous but their combination is unusual enough to create a fantastic quality: without resorting to any expensive trickery they unbalance the status quo and natural order of our known world.

Fantasy and sound

If montage, used thoughtfully, is a relatively inexpensive means of generating a sense of fantasy, then the creative use of sound can provide similarly inexpensive but potent possibilities. Sound can make the invisible visible. It can transform our understanding of the image and perception of the offscreen as well as the onscreen diegetic world. And all of this can be done through some of the basic tools of constructing meaning in film: juxtaposition and synchronisation.

Film (and other audio-visual media) is able to align the audio and visual tracks in ways that nature never intended – and in so doing it enables us to experience our world anew, compelling us to make sense of this juxtaposition and what it might mean. To make sense of these conflicting elements, to compare and contrast them and arrive at an interpretation of their relationship is to engage in metaphoric thinking. For the pioneering film sound designer Walter Murch, it is the medium's responsibility to create these metaphors:

> By comparison [with painting, music, literature, radio and so on], film seems to be 'all there' (it isn't, but it seems to be), and thus the responsibility of filmmakers is to find ways within that completeness to refrain from achieving it. To that end, the metaphoric use of sound is one of the most fruitful, flexible and inexpensive means: by choosing carefully what to eliminate, and then adding sounds that at first hearing seem to be somewhat at odds with the accompanying image, the filmmaker can open up a perceptual vacuum into which the mind of the audience must inevitably rush. (1995: 247)

One of the great champions of the metaphoric potential of the sound-image relationship is the Austrian avant-garde filmmaker Peter Kubelka. Speaking at the first School of Sound, at the Institute français in London in 1998, Kubelka related a pivotal moment from his childhood in which he became aware of the astonishing potential for the synchronisation between sounds and images. Sat in class as a little boy, Kubelka was daydreaming and gazing out of the window. As he did so, he watched a small bird flutter down and alight on a branch, with a devastating CRASH! Kubelka was amazed – what manner of bird was this? He then noticed that a car demolition yard adjoined the school and had dropped a car from a crane at the exact moment the bird landed on the branch. The effect here is the creation of what Michel Chion, one of the principal writers on film sound, calls 'audio-visual dissonance' (1994: 37). Through the synchronisation of sound and image, Kubelka's experience of reality had been transformed. As well as transforming what we do see, sound can also call into existence things that we *do not* see. The French composer Pierre Schaeffer (the founder of *musique concrète*) introduced the term *acousmatic* to refer to those sounds which we hear without seeing their source. Used in film, acousmatic sound invites the spectator to identify and make sense of its source. Acousmatic sound is used all the time in non-fantasy films to build up and expand the visible diegetic world but it is particularly effective in helping create convincing fantasy worlds. David Lynch's films, especially his collaborations with the sound designer Alan Splet on films such as *Eraserhead* (1977) and *Blue Velvet* (1986), often use acousmatic sound on the threshold of perception to create an unsettling industrial presence that we are only just aware of. For Lynch:

> Sound is 50 per cent of a film, at least. In some scenes it's almost 100 per cent. It's the thing that can add so much emotion to a film. It's a thing that can add all the mood and create a larger world. It sets the tone and it moves things. Sound is a great 'pull' into a different world. (2003: 52)

The films of Andrei Tarkovsky contain some of the most distinctive approaches to the soundtrack in all cinema including what Chion has described as a moment of 'true free counterpoint' (1994: 39) in *Solaris* when Khari (Natalya Bondarchuk) is resurrected having attempted suicide, through drinking liquid oxygen, in a desperate attempt to free her lover Kris (Donatas Banionis), and also herself, from the realisation that she is not a human but a simulacrum created by an alien intelligence. As Khari's frozen body convulses and spasms back into life we hear the sound of glass being moved and scraped but, as Chion points out, do not hear these sounds as 'wrong': 'Instead, they suggest that she is constituted of shards of ice; in a troubling, even terrifying way, they render both the character's fragility and artificiality, and a sense of the precariousness of bodies' (ibid.). Tarkovsky makes considerable use of acousmatic sound – often the source of sounds are never revealed or their revelation proves to be illogical, that is, when the source of a sound is revealed we realise it could not possibly be making that particular noise. In the strangely malevolent post-industrial wasteland that is the Zone in *Stalker* (1979), we hear creaking chains that are not actually moving – we hear the sound they might once have made, echoes of the past before whatever event that has created the Zone took place. Time is in flux and sound crosses classical temporal boundaries. In her article on Tarkovsky's approach to sound, Andrea Truppin (1992) identifies several trademarks in Tarkovsky's later films: the relationship between sound and its source; sound and space; and the use of illogical parallel sounds. Tarkovsky often uses spatial signatures at odds with what we see, adding reverberation to water drops in rooms that should be acoustically damp. For Truppin, this ambiguous use of sound encourages the audience to undertake a 'leap of faith' that is representative of the struggle with faith characteristic of many of Tarkovsky's protagonists, especially in *Stalker*. Stefan Smith notes how the use of 'discontinuous and incongruous sounds found in *Stalker* lead to what Slavoj Žižek called ontological undecidability: 'It seems as if Nature itself miraculously starts to speak, the confused and chaotic symphony of its murmurs imperceptibly passing over into music proper' (2008: 49).

Music too can contribute to a sense of fantasy. Indeed, it took a fantasy film to fully convince the Hollywood studios that audiences would accept a film with an extensive non-diegetic score (and not ask where the music was coming from). Although Max Steiner's first score was in 1931 for *Cimarron*, his bold score for *King Kong* helped cement an original score as a feature of classical Hollywood cinema. As Peter Franklin (2001) points out, music is absent from the film's opening section in 'normal' New York. It is only when the ship sails into the fog surrounding Skull Island that the non-diegetic score is introduced – the presence of 'invisible' music on the soundtrack is justified by the film's setting of a mysterious island and fantastic creatures. As with sound, musical incongruity can also call into question the status of reality in a film. Jonathan Miller's *Alice in Wonderland* makes use of a beautiful chamber score by Ravi Shankar with piano, tabla and sitar to the fore. Shankar's music makes for an odd juxtaposition – we would not expect the presence of Indian instruments such as the tabla and sitar in this quintessentially English tale of a girl in the late Victorian era. The music at first might seem inappropriate – or unreal. In his DVD commentary, however, Miller explains that Shankar's music could represent Alice's dreams of distant lands she might have heard about. As a girl in the late Victorian era she would likely be aware of the British Empire and Victoria's status as the Empress of India and so these sounds are not totally without justification. There is a tension here then between the incongruous and the justifiable – and that tension, of course, is fertile territory for the fantastic.

Fantasy films have employed spectacular effects and marvellously so but the cine-fantastic is often at its most potent when its aspects are left unseen and only hinted at, inviting us to imagine the rest. This invitation to engage our own imagination is one of the fundamental pleasures offered by much fantasy cinema. In the final chapter we will consider other functions of fantasy – including its dangers and benefits.

4   INTERPRETING FANTASY: FUNCTIONS AND BELIEFS

Why do we need fantasy? What is its function and value? The default answer, for many, is that fantasy provides us with escapism from the hardships of reality – in other words, fantasy, in this understanding of its function, is removed from and has nothing to do with reality. Instead, it offers us a carefree 'wishspace' in which we can momentarily play and relax before returning to the conditions of the real world. But is all fantasy escapist – and is escapism necessarily a bad or irresponsible thing? In the introduction, I mentioned the tendency to think of fantasy as being juvenile and immature. Such an assessment is usually founded on a refusal or inability to see beneath the surface – by focusing on people with strange hats, ears, names and artefacts we focus on the way they are superficially different from what we think of as the 'real' world. We are focusing on the semantics of fantasy without considering the implications of fantasy. In short, we are often not thinking about the difference between fantasy and reality. What happens when we contrast a fantasy world with our known world? What does that difference tell us about our world? By seeing only strangeness and then dismissing it, we often make an immediate judgement as to what it might have to tell us about our own lives – and that judgement is often a negative one. Fantasy, we might tell ourselves, is not real and so it has nothing to do with the real world and we can learn nothing from it.

But, as Rosemary Jackson has observed, fantasy 'has always provided a clue to the limits of a culture, by foregrounding problems of categorising the "real" ... it is the identification, the naming of otherness, which is a telling index of a society's religious and political beliefs' (2003: 52). Equally, to consider naturalism as being automatically more honest and 'real' than the non-naturalistic is a naïve assumption to make. Drama that appears naturalistic on the surface, in terms of costume and setting, is not necessarily more truthful than, say, a story set in an enchanted kingdom – *Pretty Woman* may look like our world but in essence it is a wish fulfilment fantasy made possible through the 'magic' of money and there is little realism in its portrayal of the life of a prostitute. Naturalism is no guarantor of truth (however we define that concept).[1] Similarly, I am not claiming here that fantasy is an inherently superior impulse for literature or drama. In his famous essay 'On Fairy-Stories', Tolkien cautioned that fantasy and its related genres can become just as formulaic and bereft of imagination as any other genre – and it can be put to negative use to repress the imagination and questioning mind:

> Fantasy can, of course, be carried to excess. It can be ill done. It can be put to evil uses. It may even delude the minds out of which it came. But of what human thing in this fallen world is that not true? Men have ... made false gods out of other materials: their nations, their banners, their monies; even their sciences and their social and economic theories have demanded human sacrifice. (2001: 55–6)

Tolkien's essay was originally delivered as a lecture in 1938 before being expanded and published in 1947. Given the timing of the essay and its coinciding with the rise of fascism in Germany, it is difficult not to connect Tolkien's comments about 'evil' and 'human sacrifice' to one of the most murderous uses of fantasy: as a means of spreading Nazi ideology, notions of Aryan supremacy and justifying the attempted extermination of an entire people. The irony, of course, is that Tolkien's own works of fantasy have been appropriated to perpetuate similar notions. Images from *The Return of the King*, the third part of Peter Jackson's trilogy of films adapted from *The Lord of the Rings*, were appropriated at the time of its release by the British National Party (BNP) as part of a recruitment campaign. Leaflets were distributed featuring Aragorn riding into battle under the banner 'Stand, Men of the West!' alongside comments (not made to the BNP) by the actor John Rhys-Davies (Gimli in the films) voicing concern about the spread of Muslim culture in the West and the erosion of Western civilisation. Tolkien repeatedly denied any allegorical relationship between Middle-earth and our world, as well as expressing his objection to the Nazi project. Similarly, in reference to his monstrous race of foot soldiers in the service of the corrupt wizard Saruman, he stressed that Uruk-ness was not a set of racially essential characteristics but were traits displayed by all peoples and cultures: 'there are no genuine Uruks, that is folk made bad by the intention of their maker ... I have met them, or thought so, in England's green and pleasant land' (2006: 90). Put like that, Tolkien's Uruks correspond more to what Christopher Booker suggests is the true function of the monster in stories: not some external ogre from somewhere else that needs to be defeated but a manifestation of our own potential internal monstrousness, that is, an expression of 'the human need to overcome the very principle of egotism, as this operates in every one of us' (2004: 582). Human nature, however, ensures that it is more convenient for us to project those traits onto other people rather than consider that we might possess them as well.

The protestations and explanations of an author do not guarantee a particular audience response. With their vivid battles and portrayal of the various (white) peoples of the West fighting for survival against dark forces from the East, the release of the Jackson films in the wake of 9/11 and the increased threat of Islamic fundamentalism made it inevitable that some audiences would relate Middle-earth to their own experience and understanding of the world, whatever the films' authorial intent. Despite Jackson's concern that the films not be read as racist, some of their visual style and intertextual references have not always helped to maintain a clear distinction between our world and Middle-earth. Scenes such as Saruman (Christopher Lee) speaking from his tower to his legions of Uruk warriors intentionally reference Leni Riefenstahl's Nazi propaganda film *Triumph des Willens* (*Triumph of the Will*, 1935) and the kingdom of Rohan is modelled directly on Anglo-Saxon culture. The filmmakers, at times, seem to want it both ways – for connections to be made between Saruman and Hitler but not to relate the image of a dark-skinned warrior in face paint riding a war elephant to notions of 'primitive' threats from the East. But how is an audience to know when such connections are intended and when they are not? Even then, the projection of monstrous or heroic characteristics onto elements of our 'real world' can take place in various ways with the same characteristics being ascribed to opposing figures depending on one's point of view and ideological beliefs. In his extensive study of the human impulse to tell stories, Christopher Booker notes how the 'Overcoming the Monster' archetype has been employed by conflicting ideologies:

> In the weeks following the terrorist attacks on New York and Washington on 11 September 2001, we saw Western consciousness building up Osama bin Laden, with his worldwide terrorist organisation, into another archetypal monster, even to the point where he was imagined directing his murderous operations from that classic monster's lair, a cave. But what we also saw was how, across the Moslem world and elsewhere, the same archetype was evoked to build up President Bush's America into an equally classic monster, heartless and blind, using its colossal power to dominate the rest of mankind. (2004: 584)

Indeed, one anti-Bush image distributed on the Internet drew explicitly on *The Lord of the Rings* in the form of a faked image that revealed the ring on Bush's finger to be none other than that of the Dark Lord, accompanied by the statement 'Frodo has failed'.

On the one hand, then, fantasy can be used to perpetuate dominant beliefs and the status quo. It can be employed to reassure its audience that all is well with their perceived world, offering idealistic solutions to society's problems. Jack Zipes has discussed how the original *Star Wars* uses a fairy tale structure to encourage and console its audience that the American system of government was still valid. *Star Wars* was made in the wake of Vietnam, political assassinations and the Watergate scandal – the result being that confidence in American political institutions had fallen alarmingly. Zipes suggests that the film reassured Americans that 'the system is all right, but that it can fall into evil hands at times … [Yet] the democratic system in America will function as long as the right people are in control, like Luke and Princess Leia' (2002: 132–3). By the end of *Star Wars* the old Republic is restored and the status quo maintained.

Yet fantasy can also fulfil a more progressive role. For Tolkien, one of the most profound and nourishing effects of fantasy and fairy stories is the way we are encouraged to look again at the familiar world with renewed wonder. Rather than taking the world around us for granted, he argues that we should learn to see it again as something wondrous, filled with possibility. This is not necessarily a naïve plea to reconnect with our inner child. China Miéville has argued that Tolkien's emphasis on the consoling function of fantasy resulted in the creation of a form of literature that 'mollycoddles the reader rather than challenging them' (Miéville quoted in Newsinger 2000). But although politically opposed to and critical of much of Tolkien's work, there are echoes of Tolkien's observation about requiring fantasy to reinterpret our surroundings in Miéville's discussion of fantasy's relevancy to our lives. In his editorial to an issue of the Marxist journal *Historical Materialism* devoted to fantasy, Miéville suggests that the cross-referencing of the real and the not-real can enable 'one to think differently about the real, its potentialities and actualities' (2002: 46). The fantastic, claims Miéville, 'is *good to think with*' (ibid.; emphasis in original).

Jack Zipes summarises Tolkien's argument as having socio-political ramifications beyond those he might have been aware of. Tolkien was strongly opposed to industrialism and in *The Lord of the Rings* that opposition manifests itself most clearly in the struggle between the Ents (the ancient guardians of the trees) and Saruman's engines and factories (the Jackson films also emphasise this theme of abusing the forces of nature in moments such as the 'birth' of the Uruk Lurtz in *The Fellowship of the Ring*, which plays on anxieties about genetic modification and cloning). Tolkien did not see fantasy as a means of losing touch with the real world but as a means of reconnecting with it. As Zipes states:

> By moving to the past or another world, the fairy tale enables readers to regain a clear view of their situations. Recovery includes return and renewal of health. The placing of objects from our everyday world in a luminous, estranged setting compels us to perceive and cherish them in a new way. (2002: 163)

Or, as Tolkien put it in his essay, to overcome our weariness and boredom with technical manipulation and clever skill (he was referring to modernist painting and drawing but that could be updated perhaps to synthetic CGI), we need to recover what we have lost: 'we should meet the centaur and the dragon, and then perhaps suddenly behold, like the ancient shepherds, sheep and dogs, and horses – and wolves' (2001: 57). It is this sense of wonder that can contribute to the escapism that fantasy is assumed to encourage.

Escapism

As we have seen, escapism, as Lucie Armitt (1996) comments, has usually been applied to fantasy as a negative constant – perceived as being about running away from the real world, shoving one's head in the sand and denying that the problems of the real world exist. Tolkien attacked this view that escapism was, *per se*, a running away from reality – that escapism was an act of cowardice. Instead, he discusses how escapism can be an act of resistance, and even heroic. Should someone be condemned for trying to imagine a different or better world? To apply Tolkien's argument to one of the pivotal speeches of the twentieth century, should Martin Luther King's dream of racial equality and civil rights have been discredited as an escapist delusion? As Tolkien asserts, when critics condemn fantasy as being escapist nonsense they often confuse 'the escape of the prisoner with the flight of the deserter' (2001: 61). If somebody stands up to and yearns to escape from their social conditions, the desire for escapism, he notes, is often driven by disgust, anger, condemnation and revolt. When escapism works effectively, it is to acknowledge the problems of the real world and provide us with the means to make sense of them and deal with them constructively. Escapism, then, does not mean, by default, cowardice and denial.

In defending fantasy from the charge of escapism, however, it is all too easy to fall into an uncritical celebration of the imagined benefits that the desire for escape might release. Ursula Le Guin acknowledges this danger in her essay 'Escape Routes' (1974–75), posing the crucial question, 'from what is one escaping, and to what?':

> If we're ... asserting the existence of a primary, vivid world, an intenser reality where joy, tragedy and morality exist, then we're doing a good thing and Tolkien is right. But what if we're doing just the opposite? What if we're escaping from a complex, uncertain, frightening world of death and taxes into a nice simple cosy place where heroes don't have to pay taxes, where death happens only to villains...? ... This takes us the other way, toward a rejection of reality, in fact toward madness: infantile regression, or paranoid delusion, or schizoid insulation. The movement is retrograde, autistic. We have escaped by locking ourselves in jail. (1989b: 179)

Le Guin's essay provides a stirring call for the liberation of the imagination and creative thought but other writers have expressed concern over the socio-political implications of escapism. Guarding against an uncritical affirmation of escapism, China Miéville questions the potential for fantasy to genuinely enable its creators, readers or spectators to escape their social and ideological circumstances in his assertion that 'precisely because you read and write books with society in your head, the "escape" that Tolkien and others aspire to is doomed to fail … the problem with most genre fantasy is that it's not nearly fantastic enough. It's escapist, but it can't escape' (Miéville quoted in Newsinger 2000). Miéville's stance on the relationship of fantasy to society is shared by Todd McGowan in his application of the philosophy of Georg Wilhelm Friedrich Hegel to science fiction cinema. As McGowan notes, whether it is a vision of a better future or a warning against a nightmarish dystopia, science fiction is nonetheless shaped by and responds to the present and its existing social structures. McGowan argues that although we 'cannot escape ideology once and for all, we can struggle against it' but to do that effectively we must reject the notion that science fiction can provide us with a portrayal of a future that is truly new (or alien) and approach it instead as a means of understanding the present: 'In doing so, we can unlock what fantasies of the future have to tell us about our present ideological deadlock' (2009: 28). In this sense, fantasy does not provide an escape from reality but has the potential to draw attention to our social conditions and, perhaps, alert us to the need to transform them.

The dissatisfaction with the real world or acknowledgement of its failings is something that fantasy has often dealt with in a subversive form – smuggling critiques of real conditions, whether they are being imposed by political regimes, racist institutions or religious intolerance, into tales that seem superficially harmless because they are assumed to be not real, assumed to be mere fantasy or child's play. Made and released in the last years of the weakening Franco regime in Spain, Victor Erice's enchanting *El Espíritu de la colmena* (*The Spirit of the Beehive*, 1973) uses a little girl's fantasy to comment on the damaging impact of the Franco era at a time when, as Derek Malcolm summarises, it was still 'necessary for Spanish filmmakers to cloak their political messages in allegory' (1999). Similarly, in his analysis of Jaromíl Jireš' *Valerie and Her Week of Wonders*, David

Melville has observed how following the 'Prague Spring' of 1968, several Czech filmmakers chose or were compelled to turn to fantasy and fairy tales in order to continue making films outside of the repressive state censorship as fairy tales were less scrutinised by the authorities. As Melville surmises, 'artists often turn to fantasy when the truth is too ugly to tell' (2007). *Valerie and Her Week of Wonders* portrays the older generation and institutions such as the Church as hypocritical and failing the young, feeding off them (literally, as vampires) and draining their energy. Jireš' film might be 'just' a vivid combination of gothic horror and fairy tale or it might be a veiled critique of the abuse of a generation denied their freedom by corrupt authorities – the film's fantasy elements enable charges of subversion to be deflected. Allegory, symbolism, fantasy and metaphor can thus provide a means of attack or articulating that which is too dangerous to voice openly.

We should, however, take care not to over-emphasise and romanticise the potential of fantasy film for subversive commentary and critique. If Rosemary Jackson has called fantasy the 'literature of subversion' we should be more cautious in using the phrase 'the cinema of subversion'. Jackson maintains that 'the modern fantastic, the form of literary fantasy within the secularised culture produced by capitalism, is a subversive literature ... the fantastic aims at dissolution of an order experienced as oppressive and insufficient' (2003: 180). Yet the nature of film production, especially those films produced by major conglomerates with huge budgets subjected to close scrutiny, means that, in general, film has less potential than literature for sustained subversion. Produced by New Line Cinema, the adaptation of the first of Philip Pullman's *His Dark Materials* books, *The Golden Compass*, omitted Pullman's critique of the Catholic Church through the analogous Magisterium, a sinister organisation who prey on the free will and creativity of children. The Magisterium remains in the film but any allusions to Catholicism are minimised. The money involved in the production, coupled with the fear of financial failure and the desire not to risk losing a potentially sizeable audience, prompted the filmmakers to alter the book's critique of the Catholic Church into a generalised critique of oppressive institutions. Genuine subversion in film fantasy, then, is more likely to be found in the work of independent filmmakers with considerable creative control than big-budget mainstream productions.

Other films have cautioned against the dangers of fantasy and mis-directed escapism. Both Billy (Tom Courtenay) in *Billy Liar* and Sam (Jonathan Pryce) in *Brazil* are frustrated with the drudgery of their respec-tive lives and dream of escape. Yet if we are initially encouraged to share their dreams, particularly in *Brazil* as Sam soars free of the bureaucratic regime that he works for, flying through the clouds to find his dream girl, by the end of each film those fantasies have been revealed as damaging. Billy ultimately takes refuge in his fantasies, preferring to live with the dream that he *might* have been a successful writer if only the train to London had waited for him, which he purposefully misses rather than risk the reality that he has not got what it takes to be a writer. Sam's fantasies prove to be even more destructive as his distinction between fantasy and reality breaks down endangering his own life and those around him, including Jill (Kim Greist), his dream girl made real. Sam fits the trajectory mapped out by Christopher Booker in his application of five stages of story structure (anticipation, dream, frustration, nightmare and miraculous escape) to those instances from history (such as Napoleon and Hitler) when people 'whether individually or collectively, are drawn to embark on a course of action based on ego-centred fantasy' (2004: 577). In Booker's trajectory, the archetypal final stage of 'miraculous escape' familiar to many stories is exchanged, in the real world, for defeat as the fantasy being acted out by the individual is 'ultimately based on defying their surrounding framework

Self-destructive fantasy: Sam's ultimate 'escape' into insanity in *Brazil* (1985)

of reality ... in an increasingly desperate attempt to keep the fantasy in being they push on, committing further dark acts, or attempting to cover up what they have done, as reality closes in [until] fantasy collides with reality, bringing about their downfall or destruction' (2004: 577–8). Unable to come to terms with his life, Sam's ultimate escape is into insanity.

A more nuanced exploration of the dangers and benefits of fantasy and escapism is found in both *The Fall* (2006) and the refreshingly thoughtful children's film *Bridge to Terabithia*, based on the well-respected book by Katherine Paterson (1977). *The Fall* is a remarkable film (not least for its landscapes and architecture) in which an unlikely friendship develops between a little girl, Alexandria (Catinca Untaru), and Roy (Lee Pace), a stuntman, both convalescing in a 1920s Los Angeles hospital. Roy gains Alexandria's trust by telling her an extraordinary tale about five mythical heroes on a quest in distant lands but exploits that trust to get her to steal drugs and medicine for him from the pharmacy. Alexandria seriously injures herself attempting to steal on Roy's behalf and a distraught Roy visits her following her operation. Wracked with guilt at the effect of his lies and fantasy adventure, Roy starts to conclude the story by killing off the heroes one by one until only one is left – the Black Bandit, who Alexandria has visualised as Roy. Alexandria pleads desperately with Roy not to kill the Black Bandit (and thus, metaphorically, not to kill himself) and it is only the strength of her emotional connection to him and his fantasy stories that persuades Roy to bring the story to a happy end and move out from his despair. Fantasy here, then, is liberating but also deceptive with destructive consequences yet, ultimately, instils the potential for redemption.

In *Bridge to Terabithia*, Jess (Josh Hutcherson) and Leslie (AnnaSophia Robb) are both lonely eleven-year-olds from different backgrounds (Jess comes from a blue-collar family with financial difficulties and has an uneasy relationship with his father whereas Leslie is the quirky daughter of two middle-class mellowed bohemians). The two strike up a close friendship around a shared love for creativity and storytelling. Jess and Leslie role-play in a magical kingdom, Terabithia, which they invent and set in the local woods. Through this creative play, Jess grows in confidence, enabling him to stand up to the school bully. But rather than simply being a homily to the power of the imagination, the film, impressively, maintains the complexity of the book and presents different positions on the balance between fantasy and reality. Having provided confidence and empowerment, Jess's escapism in Terabithia creates problems for his struggling family when it is over-indulged as he neglects his chores and loses his father's keys for work. Later, Leslie dies and Jess's initial reaction is to abandon the fantasy of Terabithia until he is able to come to terms with her death and allow his little sister to join him in the woods, as well as being reconciled with his father. *Bridge to Terabithia* presents fantasy and escapism as a healing and empowering force but one that should be related constructively back to reality rather than providing a refuge from it.

One of the most eloquent defences of fantasy film and its function can be found in a letter written (so the campaign book claimed) by Douglas Fairbanks as part of the promotional material for *The Thief of Bagdad* (1924). Ghosted or not, Fairbanks' letter outlined his reasons for producing the film and is worth citing at length:

> There is a touch of the fantastic even in the reason I made 'THE THIEF OF BAGDAD' – for it is a reason impelled by the unseen. It is a tribute to the fineness that I believe underlies the workaday philosophy of men; a recognition of the inner forces that belie the sordidness of Life. There can be no doubt that the human soul's searching for finer, higher, more ethereal things is intuitive, and first manifests itself in a child's love of fairy tales and fantasy. The dreams, longings and roseate ambitions of childhood are relegated to the background of Life by the struggle of existence, but stifling them doesn't kill them. They persist throughout the years. There are moments when we all 'dream dreams'. The brave deeds, the longing for better things, the striving for finer thoughts, the mental pictures of obstacles overcome and successes won are nearer to our real selves than our daily grind of earthly struggles. 'THE THIEF OF BAGDAD' is the story of the things we dream about, a tale of what happens when we go out from ourselves to conquer Worlds of Fancy. We set out to win our Heart's Desire; we confuse our enemies; we demean ourselves bravely; our success is complete; our reward is Happiness.
>
> I believe that this is the story of every man's inner self, and that every man will thus see it. That's the reason I made 'THE THIEF OF BAGDAD'. (1924)

The best fantasy, Tolkien believed, could offer three civilising and nurturing functions: recovery, escape and consolation. Tolkien's views on the benefits of fantasy, and indeed those of Fairbanks, are echoed, somewhat surprisingly given the three men's contrasting backgrounds and beliefs, in the work of Ernst Bloch. Although a Marxist and a contemporary of Theodor Adorno, Bloch championed a philosophy of hope and the striving for a utopian future that would free the individual. For Bloch, as Douglas Kellner summarises (see 1997: 81), fairy tales, dreams, myths and popular culture all contained emancipatory moments that anticipated a better life than the one being offered in the here and now by capitalism (or state socialism for that matter). Unlike Adorno, therefore, Bloch did not see mass-produced popular culture as merely being an empty vessel for bourgeois ideology. Rather, as expressed in his epic *The Principle of Hope* (1954–59), Bloch saw ideology as not simply being about dominating and deceiving the masses but also offering the possibility of progression and a better future. So, as Kellner explains, Bloch *would* critique a Hollywood film for its obvious political ideology – but he also believed that film *per se* 'contains much utopian potential in its ability to project images of a better life, to explore and redeem concrete reality, and to transmit utopian dreams and energies' (1997: 93). Bloch encourages a fuller enlightenment that is capable of robust criticism where necessary but is also able to acknowledge when a text possesses qualities and ideas of value, regardless of any perceived underlying ideological function. It is an uplifting vision of socialist criticism and he directed it at fantasy and fairy tales in particular. Freud might counsel against holding onto childish dreams into adulthood but for Bloch some dreams *are* important and should not be cast away as embarrassments from childhood:

> If it becomes a dreaming ahead, then its cause appears quite differently and excitingly alive ... yearning can show what it really is able to accomplish ... Virtually all human beings are futuristic; they transcend their past life ... and regard the inadequacy of their lot as a barrier, and not just as the way of the world. To this extent, the most private and ignorant wishful thinking is to be preferred to any mindless goose-stepping; for wishful thinking is capable of revolutionary awareness, and can enter the chariot of history without necessarily abandoning in the process the good content of dreams. (Quoted in Zipes 1983: 175)

So Bloch calls for a positive outlook, one which looks to the future with enlightenment, imagination and hope. If, as Jack Zipes acknowledges, there are inconsistencies in some of his writing, nonetheless, Bloch's central project, which 'focuses our attention on concrete moments in history that point the way toward an actual transformation of the material world', is one that can 'provide the impetus for individual and collective change' within the reader and viewer (1988: xxiii). Fantasy, channelled constructively, is central to this possibility for change.

Case study: Excalibur

Excalibur is far from being an arbitrary choice for an extended case study on fantasy cinema. The film was released in the vanguard of the early 1980s influx of heroic fantasy and sword and sorcery films. As a result, it is easy to view the film as being part of an opportunist trend in genre filmmaking, yet *Excalibur* is much more than a straightforward genre film and expresses instead the thematic concerns and personal vision of its director, the British filmmaker John Boorman. *Excalibur* has had mixed fortunes since its release in 1981 – the film is now something of a cult favourite but its initial critical reception was varied with often opposing interpretations being projected onto it. Many of these interpretations, however, are at odds with Boorman's stated intentions for the project and the film's own internal critique of its characters and their worldview. The film thus offers an excellent opportunity to explore the way fantasy film has been received, interpreted and used to articulate different points of view as well as to consider the dangers and benefits of fantasy.

Excalibur states in its credits that it is based on Sir Thomas Malory's *Le Morte Darthur*, published by William Caxton in 1485. Drawing on earlier sources, Malory's version of the Arthurian romance brings together the iconic elements: Arthur and Guinevere, the wizard Merlin, the court of Camelot, the Round Table, the sword in the stone, the Lady of the Lake, the sword Excalibur, the knights (Gawain, Perceval, Bors and so on), the Queen's adultery with Lancelot and the Quest for the Holy Grail. All of these elements are incorporated ambitiously into *Excalibur* and, in taking on such a task, the film occasionally sacrifices narrative momentum as it moves from one episode to another. Boorman's film, however, is no straightforward adaptation and takes considerable liberties with Malory, not least in relation to the Grail (Boorman, notably, omits the 'Holy'). As Martin Schichtman has observed, Boorman portrays a Grail whose nature is ambiguous, drawing on Christian symbolism but fulfilling a pre-Christian function (see 2000: 568–9). Throughout the film, Boorman collapses several cultural traditions into one in order to find an underlying truth that runs across differing mythologies through the presence of archetypal figures.

Where the Grail is concerned, Boorman might appear at first to be opting for a conventional Christian interpretation – as Perceval, the last of the Quest knights, emerges from the water (the baptismal allusions are difficult to avoid) and walks towards a shaft of brilliant light, the symbolism seems to be that of the Grail as Holy Chalice, and when a supernatural presence asks him whom does the Grail serve, Perceval's response, 'you my Lord', only serves to confirm our suspicions. But then comes Boorman's quite radical invention – *Arthur* (Nigel Terry) is the wounded (both physically and psychically) Fisher King figure who, traditionally, the successful Grail Knight heals on completion of the Quest, and Perceval must not ask the right question but give the right answers – which are (in Boorman's version) that the King and the Land are one, when the King is healed the Land is healed with him. What this alteration and invention achieves is to return Arthur to the centre of the narrative (in Malory he stays at home and waits for his knights to report back to him) and it also elevates him to a semi-divine status. A Roman Catholic interpretation of the Grail has it as the Eucharist, the drinking of Christ's Blood with the chalice used at the Last Supper. A Celtic interpretation has it as a vessel of plenty, belonging to Pagan Gods (the Horn of Bran from the Mabinogion and Platter of Rhylgenydd supply an unending stream of food and drink). A Ritualistic interpretation, however, roots the Grail in ancient Middle Eastern fertility rituals, centring on the death and rebirth of the God-King – which is essentially the interpretation in *Excalibur*.

It is easy to see the Grail Quest in *Excalibur* as a side-issue – it does not commence until after ninety minutes and is concluded in less than twenty minutes – and, certainly, reviews at the time were underwhelmed by it. Even the otherwise favourable review in *Variety* (which described the film as 'exquisite, a near-perfect blend of action, romance, fantasy and philosophy') suggested that if the film had a 'major fault, it's a somewhat extended sequence of the … search of the Grail, seemingly ill-established and overdrawn, threatening to give audiences itches before the picture picks up again' (Anon. 1981). Yet the presentation of the Grail Quest is fundamental to the film's philosophy. Susan Aronstein discusses how, on its initial release in the US, the film was misinterpreted and 'hijacked' by Reaganite conservatism. The perceived emphasis in *Excalibur* on militarism, the apparent fetishisation of the Knights' glittering armour (once the initial battles have been won and the Round Table is formed), the use of music by Wagner and Orff all contributed to a right-wing interpretation of the film (in Italy the film was criticised for its neo-fascist overtones):

> *Excalibur*'s initial commercial success stemmed ... from a timely release in the midst of America's swing to conservatism and of Hollywood's revival of the genre films, complete with what Susan Jeffords calls their 'hard-bodied heroes' that were the backbone of Reaganite entertainment [for example, Rambo and Rocky]. For American audiences in 1981, *Excalibur* seemed to valorise the same conservative values – the celebration of militarism, the nostalgic longing for authority, the reinstatement of the white male hero and the return of the Father ... Ray Wakefield has argued that audiences and critics in Germany read the film in just this way – as a rather chilling 'valorisation of a charismatic male leader of mythical proportions' that 'appeared on the heels of America's election of a charismatic Cold Warrior' who had 'promised to make Germany a nuclear battlefield ... if necessary'. (2005: 151–2)

Similarly, in his 1982 overview of the heroic fantasy films thriving at that time, Martin Sutton commented that the 'conventional valour and heroism' of the film, combined with its use of Wagner, contributed to an overall effect that 'would not have disgraced a Third Reich history film' (1982: 6). But, as Aronstein contends, this is a gross misreading of Boorman's film. The use of Wagner and its inevitable cultural associations with Nazism is problematic but much of the film's actual content opposes (neo) fascism. Adam Roberts argues convincingly that the initial aesthetic fascism of *Excalibur* ultimately gives way to a deconstruction of 'macho' masculinity and fascist ideology (see 1998: 111–18). Arthur is seen to be a flawed leader but one who recognises that he cannot act outside the law ('my laws must bind everyone – high and low – or they're not laws at all') and, in key moments, expresses a humility and regret that guards against an uncriti-

A warning to the militaristic: Arthur's remorse following his vanity and rage in *Excalibur* (1981)

cal celebration of militarism. When he uses Excalibur selfishly to defeat Lancelot at their first encounter and succeeds only in breaking the sword and near-fatally wounding his opponent, his reaction is one of genuine remorse at the implications of his actions:

> My pride broke it. My rage broke it. This excellent knight, who fought with fairness and grace, was meant to win. I used Excalibur to change that verdict. I've lost – for all time – the ancient sword of my fathers whose power was meant to unite all men, not to serve the vanity of a single man. I am … nothing.

The film is violent but there is no glorification of combat in the above scene and, equally, the Grail can only be won by a rejection of militarism.

Perceval only succeeds in the Grail Quest when he *casts off* his armour, in other words, when he ceases to focus on the immediate, materialistic symbol of his status as a knight. As with Robert Bresson's austere post-Grail film, *Lancelot du Lac* (1974), the knights come to worship their armour and become spiritually bankrupt in the process. In Bresson's film, the knights appear to lose their own identity as human beings – Bresson's *mise-en-scène* frequently emphasises the component parts of the knights' armour rather than their faces and, ultimately, they are reduced to a mound of scrap metal in the film's bleak conclusion. In *Excalibur*, the land flourishes when Arthur serves it and fulfils his social obligation but decays when Arthur's court falls into an idle and decadent consumerism – when he and his court lose contact with the people, the wasteland is imminent. Perceval can only attain the Grail through recognition of his failings and a selfless devotion to his community. Following his first negative review, Vincent Canby's second *New York Times* review of the film, in which he tried and failed to account for the film's popular success ('some hits defy coherent analysis'), suggested that the late introduction of the Grail Quest established the Grail as 'some misplaced lunchbox, not worth anything in itself but possessing sentimental value' (1981b). But Canby missed the point of the Grail Quest's function and its underlying mythic truth. The object in itself *is* worthless. The significance of the quest is not attaining the artefact at the end (in other words, material gain) or personal enhancement. In contrasting the respective Grail knights from Malory and Boorman, Schichtman notes that 'whereas Malory's Galahad journeys towards personal salvation … Boorman's Perceval pursues his quest for the sole purpose of saving an afflicted king' (2000: 568). The real significance of the quest is the altruistic act of committing oneself to aid another and transcending the ego. Such a process requires personal sacrifice and a series of humiliations, which Perceval endures, rather than glorious personal triumphs, if the greater good is to be served – a quest at odds with not just many of the surrounding sword and sorcery/fantasy films of the early 1980s but also the prevailing individualism of the era as well as the social and economic policies of Margaret Thatcher and Ronald Reagan.

This emphasis on the union between the land and those entrusted with the responsibility of being its guardian is essential to Boorman's reading of the Arthurian romance in *Excalibur*. Interviewed at the time of *Excalibur*'s release, he observed:

The Arthurian legend is about the passing of the old gods and the coming of the Age of Man, of rationality, of laws – of man controlling his affairs. The price he pays for this is the loss of harmony with nature, which includes magic. As we tried to state in the film, that magic passes into our dreams and is lost … The only way to regain it is by some form of transcendence, which the quest for the grail represents – to transcend the material world and find a spiritual solution. (In Schichtman 2000: 566)

In fact, the relationship between man and nature is a recurrent theme in much of Boorman's work, manifesting itself in seemingly unlikely settings such as his updating of *film noir* to the corporate culture of the late 1960s, *Point Blank* (1967), as well as more overt explorations of man's relationship with nature in his 1972 film, *Deliverance*. Boorman followed *Deliverance* with the science fiction film *Zardoz* (1974) starring Sean Connery – another work exploring humanity's separation from the natural world. Yet the project he seems to have been most drawn to was an adaptation of the Arthurian mythos and the figure of Merlin in particular.

Merlin is the key to *Excalibur*. The project's original title was to be *Merlin* or *Merlin Lives* but copyright concerns and Orion Pictures' desire for something that sounded more action- and violence-oriented resulted in a title change that does not prepare the spectator for where the film's true interests lie: 'they want to emphasise the action aspects of the story in a title that will help to sell it' Boorman pointed out pragmatically to *Sight and Sound* during the film's production (in Strick 1980: 168). The script for a much earlier version of the project, from 1975, places Merlin right at the centre of the story. In this more complex narrative (with nods to *Citizen Kane*), Arthur's kingdom is already in decline from the outset. A young Perceval is rescued by Merlin (Nicol Williamson) from a pagan sacrifice taking place at the Cerne Giant (where Merlin appears out of the Giant's mouth) and follows the weary magician. Perceval's youthful energy renews Merlin whose powers are fully restored at Stonehenge. Merlin educates Perceval and, through a series of flashbacks, relates the history of Arthur up to the present crisis, the loss of the Grail and the kingdom being usurped by Morgana le Fay (Helen Mirren) and Mordred (Robert Addie). Unlike *Excalibur*, Merlin would have had the film's final words following the death of Arthur:

> MERLIN (voice-over): The legend says that Arthur departed to the land of Avalon but he will return at the hour of England's greatest need. And the cry of Merlin shall be heard again in the forest.
>
> His laugh rings through the trees. We peer into the mysterious deeps but there is only darkness. His laugh dies away leaving the sounds of the woodland, melodious and comfortingly familiar. The End. (Boorman 1975: 134)

In *Excalibur*, however, Merlin's ultimate function is far more important than a storytelling device. He provides Boorman and the film with an exit strategy from the fascist potential inherent in both the story as well as Boorman's incorporation of a Jungian approach to his material. Boorman has made no secret of the influence of Carl Jung on his work and openly acknowledged in his autobiography that *Excalibur* was his 'Jungian interpretation of the [Arthurian] myth' (2003: 237). This adoption of a Jungian approach, however, runs the risk of encouraging the fascist readings of *Excalibur* noted earlier. If, as Anthony Stevens argues, Jung was 'temperamentally incapable of being a Nazi' and 'hostile to all political movements that sought to augment the powers of the state, for they would deprive the individual of his right to become authentic' (2001: 150, 152), Jung's ideas have often been associated with fascism. Aronstein observes how Jung's emphasis on archetypes and a 'universal vision of social and psychological health, to be found in an ordered patriarchal hierarchy, in which all things ideally moved toward their destiny in the service of a benevolent "first cause" – often symbolised in the Grail and its quest – was ... appropriated by early twentieth-century fascist regimes, particularly Nazi Germany' (2005: 153). If the portrayal of the Grail Quest as selfless devotion to one's community distances the film from the individualism of the 1980s, the realisation of Merlin provides the film with a presence and voice that actively speaks out against and undermines any tendency to fascism. To arrive at a neo-fascist interpretation of *Excalibur* is to dismiss the lessons of the Grail Quest and not pay heed to the counsel of Merlin.

As Boorman outlined, the film portrays the old world as a polytheistic one being replaced by a new order, the monotheism of Christianity. The representative of the old world is Merlin – but this Merlin seems different. We may think of Merlin as a wizened man with a pointy hat, flowing beard and spells tripping from his fingers but that image is missing here. Nicol Williamson's dynamic performance as Merlin, dancing between vocal registers, underpins the film and impressed the otherwise unmoved Vincent Canby who acknowledged Williamson's 'fine mixture of con-artistry and the detachment of a truly wise man' (1981a). Williamson's ability to shift between opposing personae ('a dream to some – a nightmare to others!') and the scripting of the character by Boorman and Rospo Pallenberg, makes Merlin less the all-powerful sorcerer and more a Trickster figure. Tricksters are recurrent figures in folklore and mythology as well as contemporary

Merlin as Trickster: 'a fool to some ...

... a nightmare to others!' in *Excalibur* (1981)

culture with prominent Tricksters including Monkey, Loki, Coyote, Hermes, Krishna, Brer Rabbit or certain incarnations of the doctor in *Doctor Who* to give a more recent example. Defining all the features of a Trickster is never easy because by their nature they change, shift and defy easy classification but there are several recurrent traits. Boorman's conception of Merlin and Williamson's performance exemplify these characteristics.

Tricksters tend to be quick-witted and fleet of foot (Merlin is certainly the former and, although he is never seen moving at anything more than a purposeful walk, he is able to travel magically about the woods and arrive, on his terms, at exactly the right moment). The Trickster is not interested in power for himself – and is usually a champion of powerless groups, undermining and subverting those who set themselves up as gods and rulers. The Trickster is both a guardian and a mischief-maker, a shape-changer and deceiver: Merlin allows Uther to take on the likeness of Igrayne's husband so that Arthur can be born. He is a maker and breaker of rules (as Merlin says, 'sometimes I give, sometimes I take – it is mine to decide which and when') capable of being gentle and self-mocking or harsh and cruel – having colluded with Uther in his deception of Igrayne, Merlin coldly withdraws his support and informs Uther of the consequence of his actions: 'You betrayed the Duke. You stole his wife. You took his castle. Now no one trusts you. You're not the one Uther.' The Trickster often operates as an intermediary between a mortal, earthly existence and the spirit world or supernatural realm and this is certainly true of *Excalibur* where Merlin's magic and power is related directly to the earth – and must be used with respect. Uttering the 'charm of making' takes its toll on Merlin and, in the film's world, magic is not unlimited but is rather a supernatural resource that should be used judiciously and not exploited (as Morgana discovers to her cost).

But as well as having access to special abilities, the Trickster is also aware of his own weaknesses, failing as often as he succeeds. When Arthur asks for advice on a mysterious knight he is about to fight (Lancelot), Merlin is fishing in a stream with his bare hands. Merlin appears focused on his prey, 'Shh! Look at him – so beautiful – so quick!' but he could just as easily be referring to Lancelot, waiting in his glistening armour (like the fish, Lancelot is 'of the Lake' and his armour has webbed joints and fins). Arthur watches impatiently as Merlin seems to outwit his quarry then, in his moment of triumph, loses control of the fish and falls backwards into the stream. Unimpressed, Arthur gallops off determined to fight Lancelot and so fails to hear Merlin's observation: 'Remember, there's always something cleverer than yourself!' It is a wonderfully multi-layered moment – the mighty sorcerer is defeated by a fish but in the same instance provides Arthur with a vital piece of advice, which he is too angry and impatient to acknowledge and proceeds to be humiliated in battle with Lancelot. Later, Merlin is undone by Morgana who traps him with his own magic – and here he is defeated by the evil that has come about as a result of his own deception. Morgana's hatred of Arthur and his kingdom stems from her desire for revenge having seen through Merlin's magic as a girl and witnessed what was, in effect, the rape of her mother, Igrayne, by Uther. For Jung, the Trickster is a 'collective shadow figure, a summation of all the inferior traits of character in individuals' (1991: 270) – and a shadow is exactly what Merlin becomes in *Excalibur* (although the Trickster is not always portrayed as the embodiment of all 'inferior character traits'). Significantly, however, Boorman changes Merlin's fate from Malory's version. In Malory, Merlin is deceived and remains imprisoned in a cave but, having had him similarly trapped and enchanted by Morgana, Boorman releases Merlin's spirit so that he lives on in Arthur's dreamworld and enters into the collective unconscious.

Why should any of this matter to us? The true value of the Trickster, I would suggest, is that they can also operate as a healing figure, not least in their ability to bridge opposing elements and thus point the way to a more balanced psyche, warning us of the dangers of excess. Western culture has traditionally been constructed on a set of dualisms: good versus evil, mind versus body (or spirit versus flesh), civilisation versus wilderness, reason versus emotion, art versus entertainment, white versus black, male versus female and so on. These dualisms, which set aspects of the world in conflict with each other, are damaging, creating divisions between cultures and races and genders or even within our own self. In dualistic thinking, the two elements are not in harmony – the former is privileged and legitimated at the expense and denigration of the latter. Put crudely, you are either one thing or the other and if you are the Other then you are in trouble. Merlin, in the Celtic tales and in Boorman's *Excalibur*, is neither one thing nor the other but embraces opposites rather than setting them against each other, something that he expresses in the scene where he leads Morgana into the caverns beneath Camelot. As John Granrose (1996) outlines, in his study of the wizard archetype, one of the stories of Merlin's origins, by Robert de Boron, has a Devil impregnating a virgin to undo the work of Christ – but the girl confesses and is consecrated with holy water so that the Devil's power over the child is broken. The child is Merlin, and so in this account, right from the start, Merlin is a fusion of opposites – a Devil father and virgin mother. Merlin deceives but he does good as a result, he is immortal but aches for mortal love. Elsewhere in the Arthurian mythos, it is Merlin who solves the riddle of the opposites, represented by two dragons beneath the earth. In the film's script he is described as 'a man without age, at once ancient and boyish, female and male'. Although that androgynous nature is not conveyed by Williamson, the fusion of opposites is expressed elsewhere in his performance. Tonal and vocal shifts aside, as a middle-aged actor Williamson avoids being the 'man with a long white beard' cliché of Merlin that Michael Torregrossa (2004: 172) curiously ascribes to him (and was Boorman's initial description in the 1975 script for *Merlin Lives*).

For Marie-Louise von Franz, the 'primal opposites which the Christian teaching has torn apart into an unresolvable conflict (e.g. spirit versus flesh) exist together in his [Merlin's] nature' (1998: 275). Von Franz's statement is less a critique of the life and teaching of Jesus Christ and more a comment on the way in which other institutions have perceived, appropriated and even misrepresented that teaching for their own agendas. Indeed, as James Conroy argues, in an essay on the Trickster in Religious Education, founding figures in major religions tend to be portrayed as figures of conservatism when the reality, certainly in the case of Jesus (a radical, intent on overturning oppression, conformity and needless ritual), could not be more different. One of the great benefits of Trickster figures, Conroy asserts, is their ability to cross boundaries, break entrenched ways of thinking and call attention to our weaknesses:

> The Trickster is one who, in the patterns of myth, legend and folk-lore narrative, moves between symbolic categories of being and action, changing shape and identity in order to expose and redress various deep-seated human follies. He ... inhabits a borderland between different worlds or different conceptions of the world and its experiential content. He is frequently a religious or quasi-religious figure who serves a ritualised function in mocking and challenging the forces of the *status quo*. (2002)

So Merlin is both of Arthur's court but exists outside it as well, coming and going as he pleases, celebrating Camelot as well as teasing it.

Depending on one's point of view, *Excalibur* is either an artistic hodge-podge of confused elements or, as Michel Ciment suggests, 'a bewildering variety of styles and periods [that] revive the Arthurian cycle' (1986: 10). The film was shot in Ireland and the Academy Award-nominated cinematography of the landscapes is lush during those scenes where Arthur's kingdom flourishes (such as Lancelot riding through a sea of bluebells) and bleak for the Grail Quest sequence. But for much of his non-diegetic music, Boorman goes as far away from Celtic culture as he can by making extensive use of Richard Wagner's late nineteenth-century music for *Tristan und Isolde* (1865), *Götterdämmerung* (1876) and *Parsifal* (1882). Yet, in terms of Boorman's project and his interest in expressing a potent mythic truth that has informed various cultures as opposed to historical truth, the Wagner pieces, particularly the prelude from *Parsifal*, are entirely logical as they draw on and respond to the same body of legends (unlike the use of Orff's *Carmina Burana* (1936), which does not offer the same level of intertextual coherence). For Muriel Whitaker (2002), however, this fusion of Celtic and Teutonic mythology renders the film inconsistent and flawed – with Celtic myth, French romance and Teutonic-derived works such as *The Lord of the Rings* and Wagner's *Ring* cycle clashing together with irreconcilable differences. That may be so but we could also argue that somewhere in the wake of such a cultural clash can be heard the chuckle of the Trickster. Lewis Hyde describes the Trickster as an 'artus worker' (from the Latin for 'joint') (1998: 256) – in other words, the Trickster encourages flexibility and cultural mobility, something that is of vital importance in an age of increasing immigration and cross-cultural encounters. If those encounters are to be exchanges and interactions rather than damaging collisions, we could do worse than draw a lesson from the Trickster. As Conroy states:

> One of the attractions of the Trickster is that he [reminds] his audience that all cultures are hybrid, implicated, and compromised. The Trickster figure travels so naturally across cultures [and] is sustained by an underlying recognition that what unifies diverse peoples is the messiness of human interaction and the consequent futility of all pursuits of the ethnically or nationally pure. (2002)

Far from being ethnically and culturally pure, the portrayal of Merlin as Trickster and Boorman's understanding of the wide-reaching vitality of the story's myth, one contributed to by different cultures through the ages, gives *Excalibur* a built-in antidote of cultural openness to help protect it from fascist interpretations and allegories. That antidote, as we have seen, is not fool-proof and the film's blood and thunder might, for some, drown out Merlin's advice and the message of the Grail Quest. The conflicting ideological readings of Excalibur underline the danger in assuming that a film has any one fixed meaning for its audiences, as certain elements, scenes and lines of dialogue can be emphasised over others in order to arrive at a particular interpretation, informed by the context of an individual's background and cultural understanding. The use of Wagner's music in *Excalibur*, for example, will not automatically signify fascism for every audience member, whereas the association between Wagner, an outspoken anti-semite, and fascism is so strong for some that the music cannot be interpreted in any other way – performances of Wagner's music are still prohibited in Israel today. Yet for all its flaws and 'fair share of silliness', as Boorman himself has described it (quoted in Kemp 2001: 24), particularly some moments of awkward acting and the somewhat lurid grotto of Merlin's subterranean realm, *Excalibur* remains a bold piece of filmmaking and a passionate statement about the power of myth with thought-provoking commentary on our social and environmental responsibilities. Having trapped him in a crystal tomb, Morgana mocks Merlin for being a fool but, as Hans Richter observed, drawing connections between the fool and the fantastic film, 'the fool who speaks the truth is a philosophical figure … in the area of the fantastic film, too, there exist possibilities of contributing to the spiritual and social life of our contemporaries, of extending, enriching and enlivening their imaginations' (1986: 63). Rather than being 'mere' escapism with no social relevancy, the Trickster/Merlin in *Excalibur* demonstrates how fantasy can critique contemporary reality and, at its very best, provide counsel and a potentially healing function to a receptive audience.

Conclusion

Fantasy film, then, is far more than a niche genre. It is one of the fundamental impulses in filmmaking expressed in a wide range of genres and cinematic traditions. Fantasy has stimulated the development of the medium itself, encouraging new techniques and technologies. As an impulse, fantasy articulates our desires and concerns, whether they are conscious or unconscious, controlling or liberating, expressing a fear of change or yearning for transformation, be it personal, political, social, sexual and so on. Michael Klossner has commented that 'a viewer who is told he is going to see a "fantasy film" can assume very little' (1999: 531) – that film might turn out to be a supernatural rom-com, a swashbuckling adventure to retrieve an ancient treasure, an exploration of childhood memories or the opportunity to step through a door into the head of a film star and experience the world through their eyes. Fantasy can and has fallen into predictable generic patterns, which, at their most informally derivative, might include reductive formulae such as: 'a wizard, a warrior, an elf and a dwarf walked into an evil kingdom to ask the overlord for a magical artefact (and he said "why the longsword?"). Then they all had a big fight and lived happily ever after'. But, as films such as *Being John Malkovich* have demonstrated, the fantasy impulse also continues to produce films quite unlike any other that defy easy categorisation and prompt us to reconsider what is possible in the medium. Hans Richter asserted in the late 1930s that 'the potentialities of the fantastic film and the grotesque film have by no means yet been exhausted' (1986: 63) and I would suggest that Richter's statement still holds true. New genres will come and go but the fantasy impulse will remain. As long as we continue to imagine, as long as we continue to desire – in other words, as long as we continue to be *human* – then we will continue to make and watch fantasy films – and, as I hope this book has justified, to study them as well.

NOTES

introduction

1 The tendency for fantasy films post-2001 to be literary adaptations
   is underlined by Leslie Stratyner and James Keller's edited collection
   Fantasy Fiction Into Film (2007), which contains essays on films such
   as *The Lord of the Rings* (2001–03), *Howl's Moving Castle* (2004), *The
   Chronicles of Narnia: The Lion, the Witch and the Wardrobe* (2005) and
   Charlie and the Chocolate Factory (2005).

chapter one

1 For full details on the UK Film Council's classification of films by genre,
   see http://www.ukfilmcouncil.org.uk/genre (accessed 3 April 2009).
2 In later work, Suvin would revisit and soften his initial hardline stance
   on science fiction, particularly in relation to metaphysical elements.
   See Patrick Parrinder (2000).
3 The Campaign Book did not stop at cushions. Exhibitors of *The Thief of
   Bagdad* were also advised to approach the 'best carpet dealer in town'
   to advertise the film alongside 'his best Persian carpet' with a card
   saying 'THE MAGIC CARPET' followed by the small print 'we cannot
   claim for it the same qualities as "The Magic Carpet" in "THE THIEF
   OF BAGDAD", but we do say that it represents the highest standard of
   Persian Carpet Maker's Art' (which must have been a great consolation
   to distraught children and harassed parents). See Anon. (1924a).
4 As above, all statistics relating to the UK Film Council's genre databases
   can be found at http://www.ukfilmcouncil.org.uk (accessed 3 April
   2009). To access the Council's Statistical Yearbooks, which also include

the box-office data mentioned here, go to http://www.ukfilmcouncil.org.
uk/10022?page=1&step=10&viewby=category&value=16998 (accessed
3 April 2009).

chapter two

1   This destabilising of Tagi's heroic status would have been even more
    pronounced had an earlier cut of the film been released. The 2009
    British Film Institute DVD of the film contains deleted scenes cut from
    the theatrical release, including Princess Dunya's daring rescue of a
    trussed-up Tagi. Disguised as a cloaked and helmeted warrior, Dunya
    frees Tagi from his captors, bears him away on horseback and then
    overcomes the villain in a cliff-top dagger-duel before revealing her
    identity to Tagi.

chapter four

1   The dismissal of fantasy as being 'not real' and therefore irrelevant to
    our actual lived conditions is noted by Elizabeth Cowie in her asser-
    tion that 'the opposition real/not real is wholly inappropriate to a
    consideration of fantasy' (1993: 147). Cowie employs a psychoanalyti-
    cal understanding of fantasy in terms of desire (as discussed in this
    book's introduction) to explore how *The Reckless Moment* (1949),
    a film set in suburban Los Angeles and otherwise categorised as
    melodrama and *film noir*, can be seen to articulate certain fantasies
    of sexual difference and behaviour. This blurring of the categories of
    fantasy and reality and the assumptions related to them is expressed
    memorably by the writer Ursula Le Guin in her 1974 essay 'Why Are
    Americans Afraid of Dragons?' As Le Guin clarifies, being anti-fantasy is
    not exclusive to the US but is a feature, she suggests, of 'almost all very
    highly technological peoples' (1989a: 31). For Le Guin, 'fake realism is
    the escapist literature of our time. And probably the ultimate escapist
    reading is that masterpiece of total unreality, the daily stock market
    report' (1989a: 34). Le Guin's observation about fake realism being the
    escapist literature of the 1970s can be expanded and updated easily
    to include the fake reality of so-called 'reality television' such as *Big*

Brother or talent shows such as *Britain's Got Talent* which encourage the fantasy that the contestants' lives will be transformed for the better by participating in a series of increasingly engineered and manipulated scenarios, enhanced by editorial decisions, accompanying music, the presenters' patter and so on.

FILMOGRAPHY

5,000 Fingers of Dr T, The (Roy Rowland, 1953, US)
7th Voyage of Sinbad, The (Nathan Juran, 1958, US)
2001: A Space Odyssey (Stanley Kubrick, 1968, UK/US)
A Canterbury Tale (Michael Powell and Emeric Pressburger, 1944, UK)
A Matter of Life and Death (Michael Powell and Emeric Pressburger, 1946, UK)
Aladdin (Ron Clements and John Musker, 1992, US)
Aladdin and the Wonderful Lamp (Chester M. Franklin and Sidney Franklin, 1917, US)
Ali Baba and the Forty Thieves (Chester M. Franklin and Sidney Franklin, 1918, US)
Alice in Wonderland (Jonathan Miller, 1966, UK)
Arabian Nights (John Rawlins, 1942, US)
Azur & Asmar: The Princes' Quest (Michel Ocelot, 2006, Spain/Italy/Belgium/France)
Barbe-bleue/Blue-beard (Georges Méliès, 1901, France)
Basic Instinct (Paul Verhoeven, 1992, US/France)
Basic Instinct 2 (Michael Caton-Jones, 2006, Germany/UK/US/Spain)
Beast from 20,000 Fathoms, The (Eugène Lourié, 1954, US)
Beastmaster, The (Don Coscarelli, 1982, US/W. Germany)
Being John Malkovich (Spike Jonze, 1999, US)
Between Two Worlds (Edward A. Blatt, 1944, US)
Beyond Tomorrow (A. Edward Sutherland, 1940, US)
Big Fish (Tim Burton, 2003, US)
Billy Liar (John Schlesinger, 1963, UK)
Birds, The (Alfred Hitchcock, 1963, US)
Blade Runner (Ridley Scott, 1982, US/Singapore)
Blue Velvet (David Lynch, 1986, US)

Brazil (Terry Gilliam, 1985, UK)
Bridge to Terabithia (Gabor Csupo, 2007, US)
Brothers Grimm, The (Terry Gilliam, 2005, UK/Czech Republic/US)
Bruce Almighty (Tom Shadyac, 2003, US)
Cat People (Jacques Tourneur, 1942, US)
Cendrillon/Cinderella (Georges Méliès, 1899, France)
Charlie and the Chocolate Factory (Tim Burton, 2005, US/UK)
Chronicles of Narnia: The Lion, the Witch and the Wardrobe, The (Andrew
    Adamson, 2005, US)
Citizen Kane (Orson Welles, 1941, US)
Clash of the Titans (Desmond Davis, 1981, US)
Company of Wolves, The (Neil Jordan, 1984, UK)
Conan the Barbarian (John Milius, 1982, US)
Conan the Destroyer (Richard Fleischer, 1984, US)
Dark Crystal, The (Jim Henson and Frank Oz, 1982, US/UK)
Dark is Rising, The (David L. Cunningham, 2007, US)
Deathstalker (James Sbardellati, 1983, Argentina/US)
Deliverance (John Boorman, 1972, US)
Die Abenteuer des Prinzen Achmed/The Adventures of Prince Achmed
    (Lotte Reiniger, 1926, Germany)
Die Blechtrommel/The Tin Drum (Volker Schlöndorff, 1978, W. Germany/
    France/Poland/Yugoslavia)
Die Nibelungen (Fritz Lang, 1924, Germany)
Dragonslayer (Matthew Robbins, 1981, US)
El Laberinto del fauno/Pan's Labyrinth (Guillermo del Toro, 2006, Mexico/
    Spain/US)
El Espíritu de la colmena/Spirit of the Beehive, The (Victor Erice, 1973,
    Spain)
Eragon (Stefen Fangmeier, 2006, US/UK)
Eraserhead (David Lynch, 1977, US)
Excalibur (John Boorman, 1981, US/UK)
Fall, The (Tarsem Singh, 2006, India/UK/US)
Fanny och Alexander/Fanny and Alexander (Ingmar Bergman, 1982,
    Sweden/France/W. Germany)
Fantasia (James Algar, Samuel Armstrong, Ford Beebe, Norman Ferguson,
    Jim Handley, T. Hee, Wilfred Jackson, Hamilton Luske, Bill Roberts and
    Paul Satterfield, 1940, US)

Fire and Ice (Ralph Bakshi, 1983, US)
Fisher King, The (Terry Gilliam, 1991, US)
Flash Gordon (Mike Hodges, 1980, US/UK)
Frankenstein (James Whale, 1931, US)
Freaky Friday (Gary Nelson, 1976, US)
Gedo senki/Tales from Earthsea (Goro Miyazaki, 2006, Japan)
Ghost (Jerry Zucker, 1990, US)
Ghost and Mrs Muir, The (Joseph L. Mankiewicz, 1947, US)
Giulietta degli spiriti/Juliet of the Spirits (Federico Fellini, 1965, Italy/
    France)
Glass Slipper, The (Charles Walters, 1955, US)
Golden Compass, The (Chris Weitz, 2007, US/UK)
Golden Voyage of Sinbad, The (Gordon Hessler, 1974, UK/US)
Gone to Earth (Michael Powell and Emeric Pressburger, 1950, UK)
Harry Potter and the Goblet of Fire (Mike Newell, 2005, UK/US)
Harry Potter and the Philosopher's Stone (Chris Columbus, 2001, UK/US)
Hauru no ugoko shiro/Howl's Moving Castle (Hayao Miyazaki, 2004,
    Japan)
Hawk the Slayer (Terry Marcel, 1980, UK)
I Know Where I'm Going! (Michael Powell and Emeric Pressburger, 1945,
    UK)
Il fiore delle mille e una notte/Arabian Nights (Pier Paolo Pasolini, 1974,
    Italy/France)
Independence Day (Roland Emmerich, 1996, US)
Indiana Jones and the Temple of Doom (Steven Spielberg, 1984, US)
Innocents, The (Jack Clayton, 1961, UK)
Invasion of the Body Snatchers (Don Siegel, 1956, US)
It's a Wonderful Life (Frank Capra, 1946, US)
Ivanovo detstvo/Ivan's Childhood (Andrei Tarkovsky, 1962, USSR)
Jabberwocky (Terry Gilliam, 1977, UK)
Jason and the Argonauts (Don Chaffey, 1963, UK/US)
Ju-on: The Grudge 2 (Takashi Shimizu, 2003, Japan)
King Kong (Merian C. Cooper and Ernest B. Schoedsack, 1933, US)
Krull (Peter Yates, 1983, UK)
Kuroneko (Kaneto Shindô, 1968, Japan)
Kwaidan (Masaki Kobayashi, 1965, Japan)
La Belle et la bête/Beauty and the Beast (Jean Cocteau, 1946, France)

La Caverne maudite/The Cave of the Demons (Georges Méliès, 1898, France)
La Cigale et la fourmi/The Grasshopper and the Ant (Georges Méliès, 1897, France)
Labyrinth (Jim Henson, 1986, UK/US)
Lady in the Water (M. Night Shyamalan, 2006, US)
Lancelot du Lac (Robert Bresson, 1974, France/Italy)
Le Manoir du diable/The Haunted Castle (Georges Méliès, 1896, France)
Le Pacte des loups/The Brotherhood of the Wolf (Christophe Gans, 2001, France)
Le Palais des mille et une nuits/The Palace of a Thousand and One Nights (Georges Méliès, 1905, France)
Le Petit chaperon rouge/Little Red Riding Hood (Georges Méliès, 1901, France)
Le Voyage dans la lune/A Trip to the Moon (Georges Méliès, 1902, France)
Lilja 4-ever (Lukas Moodysson, 2002, Sweden/Denmark)
Lion King, The (Roger Allers and Rob Minkoff, 1994, US)
Logan's Run (Michael Anderson, 1976, US)
Lord of the Rings, The (Ralph Bakshi, 1978, US)
Lord of the Rings: The Fellowship of the Ring, The (Peter Jackson, 2001, NZ/US)
Lord of the Rings: The Return of the King, The (Peter Jackson, 2003, NZ/US/Germany)
Lord of the Rings: The Two Towers, The (Peter Jackson, 2002, NZ/US/Germany)
Lost Horizon (Frank Capra, 1937, US)
Lost World, The (Harry O. Hoyt, 1925, US)
Magnum Force (John Milius, 1973, US)
Mary Poppins (Robert Stevenson, 1964, US)
Matrix, The (Andy Wachowski and Larry Wachowski, 1999, Australia/US)
Matrix Reloaded, The (Andy Wachowski and Larry Wachowski, 2003, US)
Metropolis (Fritz Lang, 1927, Germany)
Mirrormask (Dave McKean, 2005, UK/US)
Mononoke-hime Princess Mononoke (Hayao Miyazaki, 1997, Japan)
Monty Python and the Holy Grail (Terry Gilliam and Terry Jones, 1975, UK)
Never Ending Story, The (Wolfgang Petersen, 1984, W. Germany/US)
Night of the Hunter, The (Charles Laughton, 1955, US)
Nostalghia/Nostalgia (Andrei Tarkovsky, 1983, Italy/USSR)

Offret/The Sacrifice (Andrei Tarkovsky, 1986, Sweden/UK/France)
Onibaba (Kaneto Shindô, 1964, Japan)
Orphée (Jean Cocteau, 1950, France)
Otoshiana/Pitfall (Hiroshi Teshigahara, 1962, Japan)
Outland (Peter Hyams, 1981, UK)
Peau d'âne/Donkey Skin (Jacques Demy, 1970, France)
Pinnochio (Hamilton Luske and Ben Sharpsteen, 1940, US)
Point Blank (John Boorman, 1967, US)
Pretty Woman (Garry Marshall, 1990, US)
Princess Bride, The (Rob Reiner, 1987, US)
Psycho (Alfred Hitchcock, 1960, US)
Reckless Moment, The (Max Ophüls, 1949, US)
Red Dawn (John Milius, 1984, US)
Red Shoes, The (Michael Powell and Emeric Pressburger, 1948, UK)
Red Sonja (Richard Fleischer, 1985, Netherlands/US)
Salò (Pier Paolo Pasolini, 1975, Italy/France)
Shining, The (Stanley Kubrick, 1980, UK/US)
Shrek (Andrew Adamson and Vicky Jenson, 2001, US)
Sinbad and the Eye of the Tiger (Sam Wanamaker, 1977, UK)
Sinbad: Legend of the Seven Seas (Patrick Gilmore and Tim Johnson,
    2003, US)
Singing Detective, The (Keith Gordon, 2003, US)
Snow White and the Seven Dwarves (David Hand, 1937, US)
Solyaris/Solaris (Andrei Tarkovsky, 1972, USSR)
Splash (Ron Howard, 1984, US)
Stalker (Andrei Tarkovsky, 1979, USSR)
Stardust (Matthew Vaughn, 2007, UK/US)
Star Wars (George Lucas, 1977, US)
Superman (Richard Donner, 1978, UK/US)
Superman Returns (Bryan Singer, 2006, Australia/US)
Sword and the Sorcerer, The (Albert Pyun, 1982, US)
Sword of the Barbarians (Michele Massimo Tarantini, 1982, Italy)
Tales of Hoffmann, The (Michael Powell and Emeric Pressburger, 1951, UK)
Tempest, The (Derek Jarman, 1979, UK)
Thief of Bagdad, The (Raoul Walsh, 1924, US)
Thief of Bagdad, The (Ludwig Berger, Michael Powell and Tim Whelan,
    1940, UK)

THX 1138 (George Lucas, 1971, US)
Tideland (Terry Gilliam, 2005, Canada/UK)
Time Bandits (Terry Gilliam, 1981, UK)
Topper (Norman Z. McLeod, 1937, US)
Tri orísky pro Popelku/Three Hazelnuts for Cinderella (Václav Vorlícek, 1973, Czechoslovakia/E. Germany)
Trial, The (Orson Welles, 1962, France/Italy/W. Germany/Yugoslavia)
Triumph des Willens/Triumph of the Will (Leni Riefenstahl, 1935, Germany)
Twelve Monkeys (Terry Gilliam, 1995, US)
Ugetsu Monogatari (Kenji Mizoguchi, 1953, Japan)
Valerie a týden divů/Valerie and Her Week of Wonders (Jaromíl Jireš, 1970, Czechoslovakia)
Vampyr (Carl Theodor Dreyer, 1932, France/Germany)
Vertigo (Alfred Hitchcock, 1958, US)
Willow (Ron Howard, 1988, US)
Wizard of Oz, The (Victor Fleming, 1939, US)
Xia nu/A Touch of Zen (King Hu, 1969–71, Taiwan)
Zardoz (John Boorman, 1974, UK/Ireland)
Zathura (Jon Favreau, 2005, US)
Zerkalo/Mirror (Andrei Tarkovsky, 1975, USSR)

BIBLIOGRAPHY

Addison, E. (1993) 'Saving Other Women from Other Men: Disney's *Aladdin*', *Camera Obscura*, 31, 5–25.

Adorno, T. and M. Horkheimer (2002) *Dialectic of Enlightenment: Philosophical Fragments*. Trans. E. Jephcott. Stanford, CA: Stanford University Press.

Altman, R. (1999) *Film/Genre*. London: British Film Institute.

Anderson, C. A., L. Berkowitz, E. Donnerstein, L. R. Huesmann, J. D. Johnson, D. Linz, N. M. Malamuth and E. Wartella (2003) 'The Influence of Media Violence on Youth', *Psychological Science in the Public Interest*, 4, 3, 81–110.

Andrew, D. (2004) 'Foreword to the 2004 Edition', in A. Bazin *What is Cinema? Volume 1*. Trans. H. Gray. Berkeley: University of California Press, ix–xxiv.

Anon. (1924a) *The Thief of Bagdad* UK Exploitation and Publicity Campaign Book. British Film Institute microfiche. Unpaginated.

____ (1924b) Royal Albert Hall programme notes for 'The Nibelungs'. Paul Rotha Collection, Box 1, Item 5, British Film Institute special collections. Unpaginated.

____ (1925) 'Review of *The Lost World*', *Variety*, 11 February. Unpaginated.

____ (1933a) *King Kong* British Campaign Book. British Film Institute microfiche. Unpaginated.

____ (1933b) 'Review of *King Kong*', *Variety*, 7 March. Unpaginated.

____ (1938) *King Kong* re-release pressbook. British Film Institute microfiche. Unpaginated.

____ (1939a) *The Wizard of Oz* pressbook. British Film Institute microfiche. Unpaginated.

_____ (1939b) 'Review of *The Wizard of Oz*', *Variety*, 16 August. Unpaginated.

_____ (1940) *The Thief of Bagdad* Exhibitors' Campaign Book. British Film Institute microfiche. Unpaginated.

_____ (1942) 'Review of *Arabian Nights*', *Variety*, 23 December. Unpaginated.

_____ (1946) *It's a Wonderful Life* pressbook. British Film Institute microfiche. Unpaginated.

_____ (1955) 'Review of *The Glass Slipper*', *Variety*, 14 February. Unpaginated.

_____ (1958) *The 7th Voyage of Sinbad* pressbook. British Film Institute microfiche. Unpaginated.

_____ (1961a) *The Innocents* pressbook. British Film Institute microfiche. Unpaginated.

_____ (1961b) 'Review of *The Innocents*', *Variety*, 6 December. Unpaginated.

_____ (1981) 'Review of *Excalibur*', *Variety*, 8 April. Unpaginated.

_____ (1982) *The Dark Crystal* pressbook. British Film Institute microfiche. Unpaginated.

_____ (1984) Programme notes for the 1–2 December 'Thames Silents' screening of *The Thief of Bagdad* at the Dominion Theatre. British Film Institute special collections. Unpaginated.

_____ (1988) 'Review of *Willow*', *Variety*, 18 May. Unpaginated.

_____ (n.d.) 'What is Sword and Sorcery?' *Sword & Sorcery – your resource for fiction, interviews, articles, information and more*. Online. Available HTTP: www.swordandscorcery.org (accessed 4 March 2008).

Armitt, L. (1996) *Theorising the Fantastic*. London: Arnold.

_____ (2000) *Contemporary Women's Fiction and the Fantastic*. Basingstoke: Macmillan.

Aronstein, S. (2005) *Hollywood Knights: Arthurian Cinema and the Politics of Nostalgia*. Basingstoke: Palgrave Macmillan.

Austin, G. (2008) *Contemporary French Cinema* (second edition). Manchester: Manchester University Press.

Bazin, A. (2004 [1953]) 'The Virtues and Limitations of Montage', in *What is Cinema? Volume 1*. Trans. H. Gray. Berkeley: University of California Press, 41–52.

Belfrage, C. (1933) '*Daily Express* review of *King Kong*', *King Kong* British pressbook. British Film Institute microfiche.

Bellin, J. D. (2005) *Framing Monsters: Fantasy Film and Social Alienation*. Carbondale: Southern Illinois University Press.

Bernstein, M. and G. Studlar (eds) (1997) *Visions of the East: Orientalism in Film*. New Brunswick, NJ: Rutgers University Press.

Bloch, E. (1988) *The Utopian Function of Art and Literature: Selected Essays*. Trans. J. Zipes and F. Mecklenburg. Cambridge, MA: The MIT Press.

Booker, C. (2004) *The Seven Basic Plots: Why We Tell Stories*. London: Continuum.

Boorman, J. (1975) *'Merlin Lives'*, unpublished script, British Film Institute special collections.

_____ (2003) *Adventures of a Suburban Boy*. London: Faber and Faber.

Bordwell, D., J. Staiger and K. Thompson (1985) *The Classical Hollywood Cinema: Film Style and Mode of Production to 1960*. London: Routledge.

Bould, M. (2002) 'The Dreadful Credibility of Absurd Things: A Tendency in Fantasy Theory', *Historical Materialism*, 10, 4, 51–88.

Bradshaw, P. (2006) 'Review of *Eragon*', *Guardian*, 15 December. Online. Available HTTP: http://film.guardian.co.uk/News_Story/ Critic_Review/ Guardian_review/0,,1972313,00.html (accessed 23 August 2007).

Butler, D. (2007) 'One Wall and No Roof Make a House: The Illusion of Space and Place in Peter Jackson's *The Lord of the Rings*', in A. Lam and N. Oryshchuk (eds) *How We Became Middle-earth*. Zollikofen: Walking Tree Publishers, 149–68.

Canby, V. (1981a) 'Myth of Yore: review of *Excalibur*', *New York Times*, 10 April. Unpaginated.

_____ (1981b) 'Of a Hit, a Series And the Word', *New York Times*, 10 May. Unpaginated.

Cantor. J. (1997) 'The New TV Ratings Compromise: The Good, the Bad, and the Complicated', *Philadelphia Inquirer*, July. Online. Available HTTP: http://www.joannecantor.com/opednewrat.htm (accessed 20 August 2007).

Carter, A. (1996 [1980]) 'The Company of Wolves', in *The Curious Room: Collected Dramatic Works*. London: Chatto and Windus, 61–83.

Chion, M. (1994) *Audio-Vision: Sound on Screen*. Trans. C. Gorbman. New York: Columbia University Press.

Ciment, M. (1986) *John Boorman*. Trans. G. Adair. London: Faber and Faber.

Clarke, F. S. (1979) 'Best of the Seventies – Decade Recap: The Seventies 1970–1979', *Cinefantastique*, 9, 3/9, 4 (double issue), 72–3.

Clover, C. (1992) *Men, Women and Chainsaws: Gender in the Modern Horror Film*. London: British Film Institute.

Clute, J. and J. Grant (eds) (1997) *The Encyclopaedia of Fantasy*. New York: St. Martin's Press.

Conroy, J. (2002) 'Transgression, Transformation and Enlightenment: The Trickster as Poet and Teacher', *Educational Philosophy and Theory*, 34, 3, 255–72. Online. Available HTTP: http://203.10.46.30/ren/scholars/Trickster.htm (accessed 27 October 2005).

Cowie, E. (1993 [1990]) 'From *Fantasia*', in A. Easthope (ed.) *Contemporary Film Theory*. Harlow: Longman, 147–61.

Crofts, C. (2003) *Anagrams of Desire: Angela Carter's Writing for Radio, Film and Television*. Manchester: Manchester University Press.

Dixon, W. W. (ed.) (2000) *Film Genre 2000: New Critical Essays*. Albany, NY: State University of New York Press.

Donald, J. (ed.) (1989) *Fantasy and the Cinema*. London: British Film Institute.

Donnerstein, E. (n.d.) 'The Violent Content of American Television: A Three Year Comparison'. Online. Available HTTP: http://sociomedia.ibelgique.com/donnerstein.htm (accessed 20 January 2008).

Dundes, A. (1965) *The Study of Folklore*. Englewood Cliffs, NJ: Prentice Hall.

Fairbanks, D. (1924) 'Why I Produced "The Thief of Bagdad"', in Anon. *The Thief of Bagdad UK Exploitation and Publicity Campaign Book*. British Film Institute microfiche. Unpaginated.

Fisher, M. (2007) '"How Very Lacanian": From Fantasy to Hyperreality in *Basic Instinct 2*', *Film-Philosophy*, 11, 3, 74–85.

Fisher, P. (1998) *Wonder, the Rainbow, and the Aesthetics of Rare Experiences*. Cambridge and London: Harvard University Press.

Forsyth, N. (2000) 'Shakespeare the Illusionist: Filming the Supernatural', in R. Jackson (ed.) *The Cambridge Companion to Shakespeare on Film*. Cambridge: Cambridge University Press, 274–94.

Franklin, P. (2001) '*King Kong* and Film on Music: Out of the Fog', in K. J. Donnelly (ed.) *Film Music: Critical Approaches*. Edinburgh: Edinburgh University Press, 88–102.

Freedman, C. (2000) *Critical Theory and Science Fiction*. Hanover: Wesleyan University Press.

Freud, S. (2003 [1919]) 'The Uncanny', in *The Uncanny*. Trans. D. McLintock. London: Penguin, 121–62.

Götz, M., D. Lemish, A. Aidman and H. Moon (2005) *Media and the Make-Believe Worlds of Children: When Harry Potter Meets Pokémon in Disneyland*. Mahwah, NJ: Lawrence Erlbaum Associates.

Granrose, J. (1996) 'The Archetype of the Magician', unpublished diploma thesis, C. G. Jung Institute, Zurich. Online. Available HTTP: www.mythinglinks.org/magic~granrose.html (accessed 18 June 2005).

Grant, B. K. (2007) *Film Genre: From Iconography to Ideology*. London: Wallflower Press.

Gray, B. (2003) '"Bruce" Blesses Memorial Weekend with $85.7 Million', *Box Office Mojo*, 27 May. Online. Available HTTP: www.boxofficemojo.com/news/?id=1246&p=s.htm (accessed 7 March 2008).

Halligan, B. (2006) 'On Tarkovsky's Aesthetic Strategies', in G. A. Jónsson and T. Á. Óttarsson (eds) *Through the Mirror: Reflections on the Films of Andrei Tarkovsky*. Newcastle: Cambridge Scholars Press, 40–64.

Hartwell, D. G. (1999) 'Introduction: The Return of Fantasy', in N. Barron (ed.) *Fantasy and Horror: A Critical and Historical Guide to Literature, Illustration, Film, TV, Radio, and the Internet*. Lanham, MD and London: Scarecrow Press, 1–3.

Hashmi, M., B. Kirkpatrick and B. Vermillion (2003) 'Introduction', *Velvet Light Trap: A Critical Journal of Film and Television*, 52, 1–3.

Hockenhull, S. (2005) 'Romantic Landscapes: Visual Imagery in Three Films of Powell and Pressburger', *Journal of British Cinema and Television*, 2, 1, 52–66.

Holson, L. M. (2003) 'Animated Film is Latest Title to Run Aground at DreamWorks', *New York Times*, 21 July. Online. Available HTTP: http://query.nytimes.com/gst/fullpage.html?res=940DE5DB1F3CF932A15754 C0A9659C8B63 (accessed 20 March 2008).

Holt, P. (1933) '*Daily Sketch* review of *King Kong*', *King Kong* British pressbook. British Film Institute microfiche. Unpaginated.

Hume, K. (1984) *Fantasy and Mimesis: Responses to Reality in Western Literature*. New York and London: Methuen.

Hunter, I. Q. (2007) 'Post-Classical Fantasy Cinema: *The Lord of the Rings*', in D. Cartmell and I. Whelehan (eds) *The Cambridge Companion to Literature on Screen*. Cambridge: Cambridge University Press, 154–66.

Hyde, L. (1998) *Trickster Makes This World: Mischief, Myth, and Art*. New York: North Point Press.

Irwin, R. (2004) *The Arabian Nights: A Companion*. London: Tauris Parke Paperbacks.

Jackson, R. (2003) *Fantasy: The Literature of Subversion*. London and New York: Routledge.

Jancovich, M. (1996) *Rational Fears: American Horror in the 1950s*. Manchester: Manchester University Press.

Jones, H. A. (n. d.) 'Defining Sword and Sorcery', *Sword & Sorcery*. Online. Available HTTP: http://www.swordandsorcery.org/defining-sword-and-sorcery.htm (accessed 4 March 2008).

Jung, C. G. (1991) *The Collected Works of C. G. Jung Volume 9 – Part 1: The Archetypes and the Collective Unconscious*. London: Routledge.

Kelley, B. (1979) 'Peeping Tom', *Cinefantastique*, 9, 3/9, 4 (double issue), 80.

Kellner, D. (1997) 'Ernst Bloch, Utopia, and Ideology Critique', in J. Owen Daniel and T. Moylan (eds) *Not Yet: Reconsidering Ernst Bloch*. London: Verso, 80–95. Online. Available HTTP: http://www.uta.edu/huma/illuminations/kell1.htm (accessed 11 April 2008).

Kemp, P. (2001) 'Gone to Earth', *Sight and Sound*, 117, January, 22–4.

Kermode, M. (2006a) 'Pain should not be sought – but it should never be avoided', *Observer*, 5 November. Online. Available HTTP: http://film.guardian.co.uk/interview/interviewpages/0,,1940773,0.html (accessed 20 August 2007).

_____ (2006b) 'Girl Interrupted', *Sight and Sound*, 16, 12, 20–4.

Kline, S. (2003) 'Media Effects: Redux or Reductive? A Reply to the St Louis Court Brief', *Particip@tions*, 1, 1. Online. Available HTTP: http://www.participations.org/volume%201/issue%201/1_01_kline_reply.htm (accessed 14 January 2008).

Klossner, M. (1999) 'Horror, Fantasy and Animation in Film, Television and Radio', in N. Barron (ed.) *Fantasy and Horror: A Critical and Historical Guide to Literature, Illustration, Film, TV, Radio, and the Internet*. Lanham, MD and London: Scarecrow Press, 529–72.

Knowles, H. (1998) 'Peter Jackson Answers THE GEEKS!!! 20 Questions about *Lord of the Rings*'. Online. Available HTTP: http://peter_jackson_online.tripod.com/lotr/articles/20_questions.htm (accessed 3 September 2007).

Kotwal, K. (2005) 'Steven Spielberg's *Indiana Jones and the Temple of Doom* as Virtual Reality: The Orientalist and Colonial Legacies of *Gunga Din*', *Film Journal*, 12. Online. Available HTTP: http:// www. thefilmjournal.com/issue12/templeofdoom.html (accessed 24 March 2008).

Kracauer, S. (1999 [1960]) 'Basic Concepts', in L. Braudy and M. Cohen (eds) *Film Theory and Criticism: Introductory Readings* (fifth edition). New York and Oxford: Oxford University Press, 171–82.

____ (2004) *From Caligari to Hitler: A Psychological History of the German Film* (revised and expanded edition). Princeton and Oxford: Princeton University Press.

Krzywinska, T. (2003) 'Transgression, transformation and titillation: Jaromíl Jireš's *Valerie a týden divů (Valerie and Her Week of Wonders*, 1970)', *kinoeye: New Perspectives on European Film*, 3, 9. Online. Available HTTP: http://www.kinoeye.org/03/09/krzywinska09.php (accessed 26 March 2008).

Kuhn, A. (ed.) (1990) *Alien Zone: Cultural Theory and Contemporary Science Fiction Cinema*. London: Verso.

____ (ed.) (1999) *Alien Zone II: The Spaces of Science Fiction Cinema*. London: Verso.

Laplanche, J. and J.-B. Pontalis (1988) *The Language of Psycho-Analysis*. Trans. D. Nicholson-Smith. London: Karnac Books and the Institute of Psycho-analysis.

Lebeau, V. (2001) *Psychoanalysis and Cinema: The Play of Shadows*. London: Wallflower Press.

Le Guin, U. (1989a [1974]) 'Why Are Americans Afraid of Dragons?', in U. Le Guin (ed.) *The Language of the Night: Essays on Fantasy and Science Fiction*. London: The Women's Press, 31–6.

____ (1989b [1974–75]) 'Escape Routes', in U. Le Guin (ed.) *The Language of the Night: Essays on Fantasy and Science Fiction*. London: The Women's Press, 176–81.

Lewis, C. S. (1977) *The Problem of Pain*. London: Fount Paperbacks.

Lynch, D. (2003) 'Action and Reaction', in L. Sider, D. Freeman and J. Sider (eds) *Soundscape: The School of Sound Lectures 1998–2001*. London: Wallflower Press, 49–53.

Malcolm, D. (1999) 'Victor Erice: *The Spirit of the Beehive* – In the shadow of Franco', *Guardian*, 16 September. Online. Available HTTP: http://

www.guardian.co.uk/film/1999/sep/16/derekmalcolmscenturyoffilm (accessed 28 February 2009).

McCullough, J. (n. d.) 'The Demarcation of Sword and Sorcery', *Sword & Sorcery*. Online. Available HTTP: http://www.swordandsorcery.org/demarcation-of-sword-and-sorcery.htm (accessed 24 March 2008).

McGowan, T. (2009) 'Hegel and the Impossibility of the Future in Science Fiction Cinema', *Film-Philosophy*, 13, 1, 16–37. Online. Available HTTP: http://www.film-philosophy.com/2009v13n1/mcgowan.pdf (accessed 25 July 2009).

Melville, D. (2007) 'The Eccentric Carnival: *Valerie and Her Week of Wonders*', *Senses of Cinema*. Online. Available HTTP: http://www.sensesofcinema.com/contents/cteq/07/44/valerie-week-wonders.html (accessed 24 March 2008).

Miéville, C. (2002) 'Symposium: Marxism and Fantasy – Editorial Introduction', *Historical Materialism*, 10, 4, 39–49.

Murch, W. (1995) 'Sound Design: The Dancing Shadow', in J. Boorman, T. Luddy, D. Thomson and W. Donohue (eds) *Projections 4: Film-Makers on Film-Making*. London: Faber and Faber, 237–51.

Napier, S. (2005) *Anime from Akira to Howl's Moving Castle: Experiencing Contemporary Japanese Animation*. Basingstoke and New York: Palgrave Macmillan.

Nash, M. (1976) '*Vampyr* and the Fantastic', *Screen*, 17, 3, 29–67.

Neale, S. (2000) *Genre and Hollywood*. Abingdon and New York: Routledge.

Newsinger, J. (2000) 'Fantasy and Revolution: An Interview with China Miéville', *International Socialism Journal*, 88, Autumn. Online. Available HTTP: http://pubs.socialistreviewindex.org.uk/isj88/newsinger.htm (accessed 25 July 2009).

Norden, M. (1982) 'America and its Fantasy Films: 1945–1951', *Film and History*, 12, 1, 1–11.

Norton, J. (2008) 'Andrei's Childhood: Andrei Tarkovsky in Conversation About the Legacy of his Father', *Vertigo*, 3, 8, 40–1.

Parrinder, P. (2000) 'Revisiting Suvin's Poetics of Science Fiction', in P. Parrinder (ed.) *Learning from Other Worlds: Estrangement, Cognition, and the Politics of Science Fiction and Utopia*. Durham, NC: Duke University Press, 36–50.

Pierson, M. (2002) *Special Effects: Still in Search of Wonder*. New York: Columbia University Press.

Rabkin, E. (1976) *The Fantastic in Literature*. Princeton: Princeton University Press.

Ray, R. B. (2001) *How a Film Theory Got Lost and Other Mysteries in Cultural Studies*. Bloomington: Indiana University Press.

Rayns, T. (2003) 'Review of *Lilya 4-ever*', *Sight and Sound*, 13, 5. Online. Available HTTP: http://www.bfi.org.uk/sightandsound/review/1374 (accessed 4 March 2008).

Redmond, S. (ed.) (2004) *Liquid Metal: The Science Fiction Film Reader*. London: Wallflower Press.

Reid, D and J. Walker (1993) 'Strange Pursuit: Cornell Woolrich and the Abandoned City of the Forties', in J. Copjec (ed.) *Shades of Noir*. London and New York: Verso, 57–96.

Richter, H. (1986) *The Struggle for the Film: Towards a Socially Responsible Cinema*. Trans. B. Brewster. Aldershot: Wildwood House.

Rist, P. (2007) 'King Hu: experimental, narrative filmmaker', in D. William Davis and R.-S. Robert Chen (eds) *Cinema Taiwan: Politics, Popularity and State of the Arts*. Abingdon: Routledge, 161–71.

Roberts, A. (1998) *Silk and Potatoes: Contemporary Arthurian Fantasy*. Amsterdam: Rodopi.

Robinson, P. (1993) 'Is *Aida* an Orientalist Opera?', *Cambridge Opera Journal*, 5, 2, 133–40.

Rodríguez, H. (1998) 'Questions of Chinese Aesthetics: Film Form and Narrative Space in the Cinema of King Hu', *Cinema Journal*, 38, 1, 73–97.

Rudkin, D. (2005) *Vampyr*. London: British Film Institute.

Rumble, P. (1994) 'Stylistic Contamination in the *Trilogia della vita*: The Case of *Il fiore della mille e una notte*', in P. Rumble (ed.) *Pier Paolo Pasolini: Contemporary Perspectives*. Toronto: University of Toronto Press, 210–31.

____ (1995) *Allegories of Contamination: Pier Paolo Pasolini's Trilogy of Life*. Toronto: University of Toronto Press.

Ryan, M. and D. Kellner (1988) *Camera Politica: The Politics and Ideology of Contemporary Hollywood Film*. Bloomington and Indianapolis: Indiana University Press.

Said, E. (1995) *Orientalism*. New York: Pantheon Books.

Schatz, T. (1993) 'The New Hollywood', in J. Collins, H. Radner and A. Preacher Collins (eds) *Film Theory Goes to the Movies*. New York: Routledge, 8–36.

Schichtman, M. B. (2000) 'Hollywood's New Weston: The Grail Myth in Francis Ford Coppola's *Apocalypse Now* and John Boorman's *Excalibur*', in D. B. Mahoney (ed.) *The Grail: A Casebook*. New York: Garland Publishing, 561–73.

Senn, B. and J. Johnson (eds) (1992) *Fantastic Cinema Subject Guide: A Topical Index to 2500 Horror, Science Fiction and Fantasy Films*. Jefferson, NC: McFarland.

Shippey, T. (2005) *The Road to Middle-earth: How J. R. R. Tolkien Created a New Mythology* (revised edition). London: HarperCollins.

Sinyard, N. (2000) *Jack Clayton*. Manchester: Manchester University Press.

Smith, S. (2008) 'The Edge of Perception: Sound in Tarkovsky's *Stalker*', *The Soundtrack*, 1, 1, 41–52.

Spaulding, J. (2002) 'War of the Wizards: How a Ring, a Stone, and a Pair of British Accents Conquered the Universe', *Film Comment*, 38, 2, 55, 58–9.

Spector, J. (2005) 'Hollywood Roundtable: Science Fiction and Fantasy Films', *Creative Screenwriting*, 12, 4, 59–63.

Staiger, J. (1997) 'Hybrid or Inbred: The Purity Hypothesis and Hollywood Genre History', *Film Criticism*, 22, 1, 5–20.

Stevens, A. (2001) *Jung: A Very Short Introduction*. New York: Oxford University Press.

Stevenson, R. L. (2002 [1887]) 'A Gossip on Romance', in *Memories and Portraits*. Honolulu: University Press of the Pacific, 151–67.

Stratyner, L. and J. R. Keller (eds) (2007) *Fantasy Fiction Into Film: Essays*. Jefferson, NC: McFarland.

Strick, P. (1980) 'John Boorman's Merlin', *Sight and Sound*, 49, 3, 168–71.

Sutton, M. (1982) 'Sword & Sorcery', *Films and Filming*, 334, 5–8.

Suvin, D. (1979) *Metamorphoses of Science Fiction*. New Haven and London: Yale University Press.

Synessios, N. (2001) *Mirror: The Film Companion*. London: I. B. Tauris.

Tasker, Y. (1993) *Spectacular Bodies: Gender, Genre and the Action Cinema*. London: Routledge.

Telotte, J. P. (1982a) 'Editor's Note', *Film Criticism*, 7, 1, 2–3.

____ (1982b) 'The Doubles of Fantasy and the Space of Desire', *Film Criticism*, 7, 1, 56–68.

____ (1995) *Replications: A Robotic History of the Science Fiction Film*. Urbana: University of Illinois Press.

TheMrFraz (2007) 'Terrible Movie', *The Innocents* (1961) Message Board, 22 October. Online. Available HTTP: http://us.imdb.com/title/tt0055018/board/nest/88147013 (accessed 18 December 2007).

Thompson, K. (2003) 'Fantasy, Franchises, and Frodo Baggins: *The Lord of the Rings* and Modern Hollywood', *Velvet Light Trap: A Critical Journal of Film and Television*, 52, 45–63.

Todorov, T. (1975) *The Fantastic: A Structural Approach to a Literary Genre*. Trans. R. Howard. Ithaca, NY: Cornell University Press.

Tolkien, J. R. R. (2001 [1947]) 'On Fairy-Stories', in *Tree and Leaf*. London: HarperCollins, 3–81.

____ (2006) *The Letters of J. R. R. Tolkien*. Ed. H. Carpenter. London: HarperCollins.

Torregrossa, M. (2004) 'The Way of the Wizard: Reflections of Merlin on Film', in M. Driver and S. Ray (eds) *The Medieval Hero On Screen: Representations from Beowulf to Buffy*. Jefferson, NC: McFarland, 167–91.

Truppin, A. (1992) 'And Then There was Sound: The Films of Andrei Tarkovsky', in R. Altman (ed.) *Sound Theory Sound Practice*. New York: Routledge, 235–48.

Valenti, P. (1978) 'The "Film *Blanc*": Suggestions for a Variety of Fantasy, 1940–45', *Journal of Popular Film*, 6, 4, 294–304.

Various (2003 [2002]) 'Debating Audience Effects in Public', *Particip@-tions*, 1, 1. Online. Available HTTP: http://www.participations.org/volume%201/issue%201/1_01_amici_contents.htm (accessed 14 January 2008).

Viano, M. (1993) *A Certain Realism: Making Use of Pasolini's Film Theory and Practice*. Berkeley: University of California Press.

Von Franz, M.-L. (1998) *C. G. Jung: His Myth in Our Time*. Toronto: Inner City Books.

Von Gunden, K. (1989) *Flights of Fancy: The Great Fantasy Films*. Jefferson, NC: McFarland.

Warner, M. (1993a) 'The Uses of Enchantment', in D. Petrie (ed.) *Cinema and the Realms of Enchantment: Lectures, Seminars and Essays by Marina Warner and Others*. London: British Film Institute, 13–35.

____ (1993b) 'Women Against Women in the Old Wives' Tale', in D. Petrie (ed.) *Cinema and the Realms of Enchantment: Lectures, Seminars and Essays by Marina Warner and Others*. London: British Film Institute, 63–84.

Wasko, J. (2001) *Understanding Disney: The Manufacture of Fantasy*. Cambridge: Polity Press.

Whitaker, M. (2002) 'Fire, Water, Rock: Elements of Setting in John Boorman's *Excalibur* and Steve Barron's *Merlin*', in K. Harty (ed.) *Cinema Arthuriana: Twenty Essays*. Jefferson, NC: McFarland, 44–53.

Whitley, R. J. (1933) *'Daily Mirror* review of *King Kong*', *King Kong* British pressbook. British Film Institute microfiche. Unpaginated.

Wood, R. (1978) 'Return of the Repressed', *Film Comment*, 14, 4, 25–32.

_____ (2006 [1976]) 'The Ghost Princess and the Seaweed Gatherer: *Ugetsu Monogatari* and *Sansho Dayu*', in *Personal Views* (revised edition). Detroit, MI: Wayne State University Press, 273–301.

Worley, A. (2005) *Empires of the Imagination: A Critical Survey of Fantasy Cinema from Georges Méliès to The Lord of the Rings*. Jefferson and London: McFarland.

Zipes, J. (1983) *Fairy Tales and the Art of Subversion*. London: Heinemann.

_____ (1988) 'Introduction: Toward a Realization of Anticipatory Illumination', in E. Bloch *The Utopian Function of Art and Literature: Selected Essays*. Trans. J. Zipes and F. Mecklenburg. Cambridge, MA: The MIT Press, xi–xliii.

_____ (1994) 'Breaking the Disney Spell', in *Fairy Tale as Myth, Myth as Fairy Tale*. Lexington: University of Kentucky Press, 72–95.

_____ (1997) *Happily Ever After: Fairy Tales, Children and the Culture Industry*. New York and London: Routledge.

_____ (2002) *Breaking the Magic Spell: Radical Theories of Folk and Fairy Tales*. Lexington: University of Kentucky Press.

Žižek, S. (1991) *Looking Awry: An Introduction to Jacques Lacan Through Popular Culture*. Cambridge, MA: The MIT Press.

_____ (2001) *The Fright of Real Tears: Krzysztof Kieślowski Between Theory and Post-Theory*. London: British Film Institute.

Zucker, C. (2000) '"Sweetest Tongue has Sharpest Teeth": The Dangers of Dreaming in Neil Jordan's *The Company of Wolves*', *Film and Literature Quarterly*, 28, 1, 66–71.

INDEX